MOTHER NATURE'S HANDBOOK

Secrets for Thriving Indoor Plants

FOREWORD

In recent years, plant growers and importers from all over the world have been providing an endless stream of plant varieties that are suitable for indoor culture. House plant enthusiasts have eagerly welcomed these exotic additions into their homes. The beauty of a plant is appreciated best when it is thriving and producing its most luxurious foliage. Revealed between these pages are Mother Nature's most closely guarded secrets.

The basic fundamentals of indoor gardening are fully illustrated with easy to follow photographs. An extensive collection of 344 popular house plants comprise Mother Nature's Family Album. Individual cultural requirements are provided for each plant.

The objective of this book is to present essential knowledge in an interesting and fun manner. Learning, in this way, will be an effortless and enjoyable experience. We hope that this book will open new dimensions for both amateur and experienced house plant lovers.

James E. Gick

INDEX

Published by
FUTURE CRAFTS TODAY

Copyright © 1976 Gick Publishing Inc.
Laguna Hills, Calif.
92653
Printed in U.S.A.

WHERE DO THEY COME FROM?

BROMELIADS

House plants are those which are capable of growing under the conditions existing in the average house. Generally speaking, and considering all types of plants, most homes or apartments are rather dark growing grounds. Therefore, plants that are commonly grown indoors are usually those whose ancestors were limited, perhaps by dense overhead growth, to lesser amounts than full sunlight. Most house plants that are sold through retail outlets have been propagated and grown specifically for cultivation indoors. Few plants that are available in stores have been collected, in the wild, from their natural locations.

CHLOROPHYTUM

Be selective when buying plants. Two major factors effect the eventual appearance of a plant; the care that it has had and the care that it will receive in the future. The past will be rather evident in the appearance and the future is up to you. Stay away from unhealthy plants. Check very carefully for pests before buying. The plants shown above, were purchased from different sources, all in the same day, and each for the same amount of money.

BROMELIADS

SAINTPAULIA

The recent increase in the popularity of house plants has created unusually widespread availability. Nurseries, plant boutiques, florists and even super markets are all excellent sources. Judge your source by the appearance of the plants and the overall cleanliness of the establishment. Nurseries and plant boutiques usually offer a very wide selection of different varieties. As is evident in the photos above, there are also many nurseries that specialize in particular types of plants.

NATURE'S TOUGHEST PLANTS

Most all types of cacti make unique window plants. They require little maintenance and are very forgiving. In addition to growing in unusual and geometric shapes, most cactus produce very lovely flowers.

Philodendrons and Scindapsis are undoubtedly among the toughest of all house plants. The small leaved trailing varieties will withstand very low light and poor watering conditions. These qualities make the plants suitable for growing in bathrooms where there is only a very small window.

The Cissus and Hedera ivies offer a wide selection of hardy decorator plants. "Grape Ivy" and "Needlepoint Ivy" are the most popular of these groups. The Cissus ivies are most often hanging or trailing plants while the Hedera ivies are capable of climbing with aeriel roots.

Syngoniums are often referred to as "Trileaf Wonders" or "Arrowhead Plants." They almost seem to thrive on abuse. They will grow in poor sunlight conditions. Pinching back the growing tips and occasionally turning the plant will result in nicely shaped full growth.

Asparagus ferns make very attractive house plants. They are easy to care for and very durable. The Sprengeri fern's long stalks arch rather than hang and grow small white flowers. The stalks on the Plume Asparagus can reach a height of 2 ft. Both are well suited for hanging pots or baskets. They require abundant and even direct sunlight.

With the exception of perhaps the "Boston Fern," tropical palms have been the most popular decorator plants for many years. There are several different types of very sturdy shade loving palms that are suitable for indoor culture. Most palms are tolerant of somewhat lower sunlight conditions and rarely suffer from the soil being allowed to become too dry.

Dracaenas are cane-stemmed plants that are rather palm-like in appearance. They drop their lower leaves as new ones form at the top. This results in a bare and sometimes snaky stem which is often considered artistic. Though they are very tough plants, they can become leggy if grown in insufficient sunlight. They also cannot tolerate wet, soggy soil.

Bromeliads are some of the most fascinating and decorative house plants available. They are easy to maintain and have beautiful coloring and leaf designs. Their flowers are nothing less than spectacular. They are classed as succulents and can tolerate a wide range of climatic conditions. They prefer filtered sunlight and moist soil.

MAINTENANCE

Regular maintenance checks should be made to insure continuous and proper growth. To keep your plants healthy and in top condition, be aware of their individual needs. This may avoid setbacks or perhaps even the total loss of a plant.

1. Locate your plants where they will receive the proper amount of sunlight. Remember that excessive amounts of sunlight can be as harmful as inadequate amounts.

2. Water thoroughly and as often as necessary to keep the soil properly moistened.

3. Provide the proper humidity needed to maintain luxurious and healthy foliage. Dry air or central heating drafts can cause the foliage of many plants to turn brown.

4. Fertilize regularly to encourage continuous and vigorous growth. Plants require nutrients, just the same as people, in order to thrive.

5. Leaching is a method of cleansing and rejuvenating the soil of a plant, without removing it from the pot. This is also a cure for many ailments of the soil.

6. Transplant or repot as often as necessary. Many plants enjoy being slightly crowded but few will continue to show

new growth if totally root bound.

7. Watch for signs of pests. Yellowing or drying leaves are usually the first indications of infestation. Mealy bug shown is enlarged 10 times.

8. Air layer or cut back spindly growth.

9. Many plants require pinching back of terminal growth to encourage branching, bushiness and full, compact growth.

10. Remove superfluous or spent blooms. Insignificant blooms, such as those of *Coleus* and *Plectranthus* do not add to the appearance of the plant yet drain considerable amounts of energy from the growth of the foliage.

11. Wipe the foliage regularly with a damp cloth. Dirty leaves can attract insects and encourage disease as well as detract from the appearance.

12. Attractive plants look their very best when potted in complementary containers. The soil may also be dressed or concealed, if desired, with the use of moss, gravel or pieces of bark.

By regularly completing these steps to good maintenance you should be rewarded with a collection of healthy, happy house plants.

LIGHT

SUNLIGHT

Providing the proper amount of sunlight for your plants is one of the most important steps toward good gardening. It can be equally as harmful to supply your plants with excessive amounts of sunlight as it is to supply them with inadequate amounts. The different quantities of light required for various plants are referred to as Low, Medium and High. Use the situations described below as guides to determine what the light conditions are in your home. Light that has passed through a sheer curtain or non-opaque type window shade is referred to as filtered light.

LOW LIGHT

Filtered light from a small window across the room.
Light from a shaded window.
Filtered light to a North window.
Light that has reflected around a wall or divider.
Indirect, yet strong enough sunlight to cast a shadow.

MEDIUM LIGHT

Bright, indirect or filtered sunlight.
A close, direct exposure to a North or East window
Two to four hours of direct sunlight per day.

HIGH LIGHT

Indirect exposure to a West window.
Long hours of good light from a South window.

Most house plants are of a tropical nature and do not grow well in hot, direct sunlight. Those that do grow in high amounts of sunlight should not be located too close to the window as the glass will magnify the heat and possibly cause sunburn.

Many plants are able to retain their healthy appearance for many months with insufficient sunlight before showing ill symptoms. Plants that do not receive enough light will grow at a slow rate and new growth will appear weak, small and distantly spaced. The plant may even start to drop its older leaves if the problem is not corrected.

Plants with color variegations or white areas on their leaves require more sunlight than their solid green counterparts. This is because of the absence of chlorophyll in the lighter areas.

ARTIFICIAL LIGHT

A whole new aspect in indoor gardening can be created with the use of fluorescent or plant growth light tubes. In recent years, several light manufactuters have produced light tubes that emit a high intensity of the red and blue color bands of the light spectrum. Primarily, plants use these two wave lengths to carry on photosynthesis, the process that they use to produce growth energy. The amount of light per day (photoperiod) and temperature, which you control, can cause flower-

Courtesy of G.T.E. Sylvania

Courtesy of H. L. Hubbell Inc.

ing plants to bloom out of season, if desired. Most house plants develop luxurious foliage when grown under these lights. Plant enthusiasts are often amazed with their new found success with gardening under artificial sunlight. The plant growth light tubes are manufactured in the same sizes as regular fluorescent lights, therefore the same fixtures can be used. For growing plants in a basement or garage, plain commercial fixtures are probably adequate. If you prefer the lights in the living area of your home, there are many beautiful and functional fixtures that are available.

FOR BEST RESULTS:
Provide 15 lamp watts per square foot of growing area. A four foot, double tube fixture, will produce enough light for approximately 5 square feet of growing area. The light is strongest and most intense toward the center of the tube. Keep the light source 12 to 15 inches above the plant tops. Supply 12 to 18 hours of light per day for most plants. Replace tubes when black areas appear near the ends. Plants should be provided with a regular resting period of no light and a slightly lower temperature such as would occur during the night in its native habitat.

WATERING

WATERING (pots with drain holes.)

Whether you prefer to top water or bottom water your plants, you should water thoroughly. The soil should be saturated with water and allowed to drain into the saucer or sink. Moistening only the top portion of the soil can result in poor root structure and growth. See page twenty for watering plants that are in containers without drain holes. How often you must water your plants is determined by many factors; size and porosity of container, the temperature and the amount of air circulation in the room and the amount of water the plant consumes. Most *Ferns, Begonias* and *African Violets* require constantly moist soil. Moist does not mean dripping wet at all times. Keep the soil moist enough so that it will pack and hold together neatly if squeezed in your hand. Constantly wet soil is not appreciated by many plants and could cause "root rot" or decay. Most *Cacti* and *Succulents* enjoy slightly dry periods of a week or so between waterings. Most house plants fall into the slightly moist to moist soil category.

Distilled or rainwater is the best for plants as it is the purest and cleanest. However, distilled water is usually not economically feasible to use and few people have facilities for holding quantities of rainwater. Tap water, warmed to room temperature, is suitable for watering. Do not use water that has been run through a water softener. To aid in moistening the soil, and to discourage pests, add 10 drops of bio-degradable detergent to each gallon of water used to water your plants.

TOP WATERING is accomplished by adding water to the surface of the soil until it flows out of the drain hole. A space between the soil and the pot may form if the soil has been allowed to become excessively dry and may make top watering ineffective.

BOTTOM WATERING is used for watering a group of plants in a single tray or for soaking a dry root mass. Fill the tray with water. Allow the soil to soak the water up through the drain hole until the surface is moist. Remove excess water from the saucer when finished.

The best guide for determining when your plants should be watered is to place your finger into the soil surrounding the plant. If the soil is hard and dry, the plant should be watered.

Recent technology has produced many types of moisture sensing devices. The battery operated types, when placed in the soil, will give an accurate reading of the moisture content. These aids can be valuable to those that plant in pots without drain holes.

Vacations always pose the problem of "Who will take care of my plants?" Your house plants can be kept moist for weeks by preparing them in the following manner.

Water the plant thoroughly and allow the excess to drain into the sink.

Place both the pot and the plant into a plastic dry cleaning bag.

Blow up the bag with air and tie securely with a rubber band.

By placing your plant in the bag, you have actually created a temporary terrarium which will contain the essential moisture.

HUMIDITY

Plants generally grow better when the humidity of the room is 30 to 50%. In a temperate climate the humidity in a home is generally between 25 and 30%. This percentage can drop in winter when the air is dried out from heating. There are several ways that you can increase the humidity; moss sticks, misting, group several plants together or use a humidifier. The humidifier is quite an investment, but the results can be very rewarding. A plastic or glass enclosure, whether it be a sandwich bag or a terrarium, will increase the humidity around the plant considerably.

High humidity is very essential to the success of propagating with slips and cuttings. After rooting plants under humid conditions, gradually "wean" them to the normal room conditions for only a few hours at a time over a period of a couple of days.

Practically all *Ferns, Maidenhair* especially, grow best under humid conditions. This is an indication that these are rather fragile plants and care should be taken that they are not exposed to hot, direct sunlight.

Most high humidity plants will benefit from misting. Spray bottles are available in most nurseries. As a general rule, plants with hairy or fuzzy foliage do not respond favorably to misting.

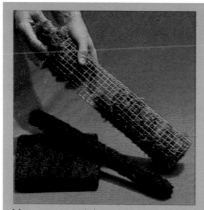

Use moss sticks to increase the humidity for plants that vine. Form hardware cloth or chicken wire into a tube and stuff with Sphagnum moss. Plant the moss stick in the soil near the plant and keep moist.

Place a pot or pots on a water-proof tray filled with pebbles. Fill the tray with water to just below the bottom of the pot. The evaporating water will add moisture to the air in the immediate area.

LEACHING is a method of washing salt and other harmful minerals from the soil. This should be done every 4 to 12 months, depending upon the condition of the water being used. Place the pot in a sink filled with water to the level of the soil. Let stand for 30 minutes or until the soil mass is completely saturated. Drain the water from the sink. Wash the plant allowing plenty of water to flow down through the soil and out the drain hole in the bottom of the pot. In addition to removing harmful minerals from the soil, leaching can also be used to correct an over-fertilized soil condition or soil that has been heavily exposed to insecticides.

SOIL

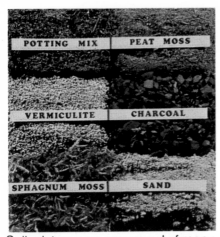

Soil mixtures are composed of many ingredients, each of which perform a function that will contribute to the plants healthy growth. Some materials are added to retain moisture and some are used for faster drainage depending upon the plants particular needs.

Cacti and *Succulents* are capable of storing large quantities of water and require very little moisture. They prefer fast draining soil blended of equal parts coarse sand and your regular potting mix. Fertilize *Cacti* only once or twice annually.

SOIL

Potting soil mixtures are available from your local nursery. Most of these mixtures have been Pasteurized or sterilized to kill fungi and insects and to discourage disease. They are also blended to fill the requirements of practically all house plants. A good potting mixture should consist of equal parts of soil, peat moss and sand. Washed, coarse builders sand can be added to the mixture for faster drainage. Vermiculite or Perlite may also be blended with the soil to provide faster drainage and a lighter consistency of potting soil. Peat moss is used to help retain moisture for longer periods. Sphagnum moss helps to retain moisture and also has many decorative applications. Activated charcoal can be used in the bottom of containers without drain holes or in terrariums to help prevent the soil from souring. Whatever soil mixture you use, it should be moistened the day prior to using. There is less chance of damaging roots when potting in moist soil. Most soil mixes are packaged in plastic bags. Seal the bag after using and it will always have the proper moisture content. Since the quality of your soil plays such an important roll in the future life of your plant, the use of soil from your yard should be discouraged unless the soil is of unusually good quality. It is very easy to introduce pests and diseases to your house plants by using soil from your yard.

Epiphyte plants or plants which normally grow out of soil in nature such as *Staghorn Ferns* and many *Bromeliads* can be planted in sphagnum moss that is wired to a piece of wood or fern bark.

Many bromeliads are epiphitical and use their roots primarily as an anchor. They absorb much of their moisture through their leaves from a reservoir of water in the center of the plant. If your plant has a center "tank," keep it supplied with water at all times.

FERTILIZERS

A regular feeding schedule is very important to having healthy, growing plants. Fertilizers are available in many forms: tablet or granule which is placed near the edge of the pot and partially dissolved with each watering; dry can be mixed with the soil or dissolved in water; and liquid is mixed with water. Fish emulsions can be substituted every once in a while in place of your regular fertilizer if desired. There are also several brands of hormones and vitamins that may be used when watering to stimulate new growth and bloom. Regardless of the type of brand that you use, follow the manufacturers directions exactly. Over fertilizing can burn and even kill your plant. Do not fertilize seedlings until they are two to three weeks old. Do not fertilize sick or diseased plants unless you have determined that a lack of feeding is the problem. Do not fertilize a plant that needs watering as the fertilizer will be immediately absorbed into the plant, and quickly will show the effects of a concentrated dosage. Feeding should be decreased to half doses and discontinued completely for some plants during colder or winter months. This will give the plants a dormant or normal resting period. As a general guide, fertilize once per month March through September. Then fertilize only every other month October through February.

TRANSPLANTING

HOW TO TRANSPLANT

(1) To remove a plant from its pot, place your fingers around the stem at the soil level and turn the pot over. Tap the pot rim on the table edge. The plant and soil should slide out of the pot.

Transplanting or repotting should be done only when necessary. *Boston Ferns, African Violets* and many other plants do not develop their most luxuriant and full foliage until they become somewhat "root bound." Some good indications that your plant is in need of repotting is when the roots grow out of the drain hole or when growth has become very slow. Poor drainage is also a pretty sure sign of cramped roots. Some plants such as *Orchids* may require repotting only every three years, whereas, a vigorously growing *Asparagus Fern* (opposite page) could consume its entire soil mass in only one year.

(2) Prepare the pot for drainage as described in the diagram. Spread a layer of soil around in the pot. Loosen the roots of the plant and position it in the pot leaving room at the top for watering.

(3) Add soil around the roots and tamp lightly with your fingers. Water the plant thoroughly to settle the soil. Tapping the bottom of the pot gently on a solid surface will also aid in packing the soil.

Clay pots are the ideal containers for most all plants. Plastic or glazed pots also work well if you provide good drainage. Containers without drain holes should be avoided unless you are sure of not overwatering. See page twenty for planting in containers without drain holes. When repotting, increase the size of the pot by approximately two inches in diameter. House plants, when mature, can be potted back into the same size container after loosening the roots and removing a portion of the old soil. Water your plant a day prior to repotting. This will loosen the soil and help prevent shock due to root damage.

DRAINAGE

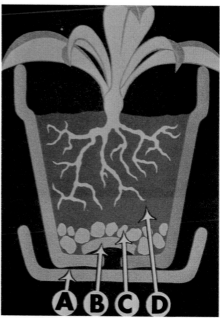

Proper drainage can be insured by following these steps. (A) Pots with drain holes and glazed saucers are best. (B) Place an irregular piece of broken clay pot over the hole to hold the pebbles. (C) Add a layer of pebbles, Vermiculite, charcoal or gravel to aid drainage. (D) Use the recommended mixture of quality potting soil.

Poor drainage means disaster to most plants. When excess water is not able to drain out of a pot, it can have the same effects as that of a stagnating pond. The soil will sour and rot the roots of the plant. The root system of a plant requires a continuous supply of oxygen in order to survive. When a pot of soil remains full of water, the oxygen supply is cut off. Insufficient drainage can be caused by three factors; a "pot bound" root system that is plugging the drain, a pot not prepared for drainage as described or a poor soil mixture.

WATER CULTURE

SYNGONIUM

SYNGONIUM

PILEA & HEMIGRAPHIS

CHLOROPHYTUM

Water culture or cultivation without soil has been practiced for hundreds of years. Not speaking of the new hydroponic techniques, but rather of simply growing plants in drainless, water filled containers. Many gardening enthusiasts, while propagating plants, have discovered that they can not only root some types of cuttings in water but can actually grow the plants in water. The advantages of growing plants in water instead of soil are: less frequent waterings are required and the plant will never become infested with soil borne insects. The drawbacks to cultivation in this manner are that most plants experience a slowed rate of growth. Regardless of the pros and cons, it can be fun to experiment and try something different in the way of indoor gardening. A few of the plants that adapt well to water culture are shown on this page. Other suggested types are recommended on pages 43 through 142. Plants that are to be grown in water should be started from cuttings. Roots with soil, if submerged in water for a period of time, may sour, producing a foul odor and death to the plant. Jars, vases, glasses or even bottles can be used as containers. Plain tap water with a very slight amount of fertilizer is adequate. Replenish the water supply as it is consumed and change completely approximately every 2 to 4 weeks. Vermiculite, perlite or decorative pebbles may be used, if desired, inside the containers to conceal the roots or to help hold the cuttings in position while rooting. Keep water filled containers, especially glass, out of hot direct sunlight.

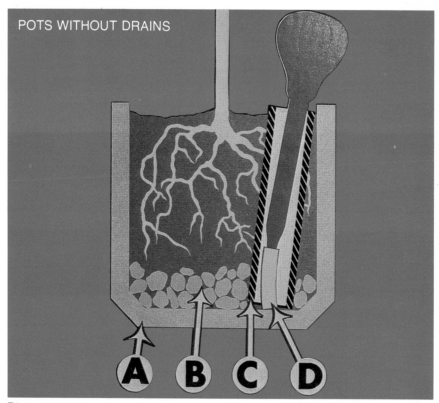

POTS WITHOUT DRAINS

Plants can be successfully grown in glazed, drainless containers. The proper watering of plants in containers of this type can be accomplished in several ways. A moisture sensing device, such as the one shown on page 3, may be used to read the moisture content of the soil at the bottom of the pot. Longer versions of these devices are available for deep pots. If the container and plant are not too large, the excess water may be poured into the sink. Most soils will remain intact if this is done carefully. The diagram above shows a popular method of removing excess water without having to move the container. A. A glazed, drainless container. C. Position pipe on the bottom of the container at an angle. The plastic pipe, such as the type used for plumbing, should touch the bottom of the container and be high enough so that the soil will not fall inside. B. Add a 2 inch layer of pebbles, rocks or pea gravel for drainage. D. A basting syringe is used to retrieve the excess water at the bottom of the pipe. A piece of rubber tubing can be used as an extension on the syringe, if necessary.

CONTAINERS

Inexpensive clay pots are ideally suited for growing plants. They are porous which aids drainage and provides oxygen to the roots. Stoneware and plastic pots also make excellent containers. They are not porous and therefore require less watering than the clay types.

Disguising unattractive or clay pots is easy. Most nurseries handle decorative containers that are made to conceal the original plant pots. Many of these containers are waterproof and will eliminate the need for a glazed saucer.

There are many watering aids available that allow you to water less frequently. The type, in foreground, transfers the water to the pot by capillary action, through a wick. The other has a large reservoir that surrounds the pot and is uniquely controlled by a vacuum principle.

Plant hangers can be quickly assembled from ordinary rope. Use three pieces of equal length. Tie them together at each end with overhand knots. Fit the planter between the ropes, above a knot, and hang from a hook.

Mossed baskets make very attractive hanging containers as plants can be grown in the sides as well as the top. They are available in many different sizes and shapes. The larger the basket, the less frequent waterings are necessary. Use 2 inch size plants for the sides of the basket. Provide enough plants so that the basket will appear only slightly full with foliage.

Spread the top wires of the basket and stuff full with sphagnum moss to form a solid and uniform collar. Straighten the wires to secure the collar in place. Pack a generous layer of moss around the inside of the basket. Overlap the edges to prevent the loss of soil when watering.

Remove most of the soil from the roots of your plants. Gently squeeze the root mass into a small, compact lump. By making holes in the moss with your fingers and by spreading the wires, insert the roots of the plants well into the basket. Straighten the wires and be sure that there are no leaks, in the moss, around the plants.

Add soil to the inside of the basket. Arrange the roots of the plants into the soil while filling. Plant the top of the basket with several small plants or a larger, single specimen. Water thoroughly when finished. Baskets must be watered outdoors or in a sink where they can drain.

TERRARIUMS

Terrariums and bottle gardens are humid enclosures that are made of glass or plastic. They provide a very tropical atmosphere suitable for growing delicate or moisture loving plants. Terrariums have been around for over a century. They have been referred to as bottle gardens, fern cases and "Wardian Cases." The discovery of the terrarium is credited to Dr. Nathanial Ward, who discovered a bottle containing soil and growing plants, while on a walk in the woods. He elaborated on this concept and made glass cases for the transportation of plants during sea voyages. Once plants are established and growing under this controlled environment, they are practically maintenance and pest free. Bottles, large brandy snifters, aquariums, and large apothecary jars are all excellent containers for terrariums. Desirable containers are those that contain the humid atmosphere, have growing room, and are clear enough to admit sufficient sunlight. Plants that adapt well to life in a terrarium offer a huge selection. Plants that enjoy misting and those that prefer a medium to high humidity should all do well inside a terrarium. Locate only in filtered or indirect sunlight. Use activated charcoal in the bottoms of terrariums to prevent the soil from souring. Use sterilized potting soil and keep barely moist. The greatest contributor to unsuccessful terrariums is over-watering. Condensation on the sides of terrariums or bottle gardens especially, is normal.

Many of the tropical plants available will grow well only in terrariums, bottle gardens or in other areas of high humidity. A fluorescent fixture has been mounted in the lid of this terrarium which would enable the plants to grow even if it is located where it receives low light. You may even have an old aquarium stored away somewhere in your garage that could be used effectively as a terrarium. Swap meets and garage sales are excellent sources for containers of these types.

FLOWERS

Most all house plants are capable of blooming with the exception of Ferns which reproduce asexually. Some plants are very easy bloomers and often bloom almost continuously with little or no effort. Others are stubborn and almost refuse to bloom indoors.

Flower forms and colors vary drastically from species to species. Bromeliads and Orchids are often extremely showy and exotic bloomers. Most Gesneriads (Saintpaulia and Sinningia) are easy

and almost constant bloomers if conditions are favorable.

The secret to causing a plant to bloom can be very complicated. The major factors to initiating blooms are: (1) hour length and intensity of sunlight; (2) temperature; (3) watering; (4) fertilizer; (5) condition of the root system.

Plants that are flowering generally require more sunlight and water than those which are not in order to continue blooming.

HOW & WHERE TO DISPLAY PLANTS

Arrange your plants in your home as decorative pieces. Place them where they will remain healthy and yet compliment their surroundings.

This lovely arrangement of Needlepoint Ivy was grown to the size shown from a stem cutting in less than one year. Some plants will grow more quickly than others depending upon light conditions, where it is located and the amount of water and nourishment it receives. See pages 43 thru 142 for the most desirable conditions for many common plants.

The Sweet Potato Plant is ideal for do-it-yourself indoor or beginning gardeners. It requires very little attention and costs close to nothing to grow. See page 104 for detailed instructions.

Grape Ivy is a hearty plant and is recommended for beginning gardeners. The plant above receives a medium amount of filtered sunlight from an East window.

Most plant enthusiasts started with only one or two small plants that they picked up at the supermarket while shopping. In the months following this initial purchase, the plants will generally receive good care and produce new growth. By this time, it is very likely that this person has been bitten by the "plant bug." New purchases, gifts and cuttings will soon increase the size of the collection to a point where the plant enthusiast won't know what to do with them all. Many plants can be grouped together if they are planted in pots that compliment each other. In fact, plants that are grouped together will often grow better than those that are separated because of the added humidity in the immediate area.

The new macrame' trend has been very beneficial to plant collectors. Macrame' is the art of decorative rope knotting. Simple inexpensive materials such as jute or yarn can be quickly transformed into gorgeous, decorative pot hangers. Very little skill is required for macrame' and the basic techniques can be learned in minutes. Interesting and unusual objects such as wood or beads can be incorporated into your hangers for a unique effect. The materials for macrame' are available through most all craft and hobby shops and many garden centers. Instruction books for macrame' are often available through the same sources. The hangers on these pages have been reproduced from HP-452 "More Macrame'."

PROPAGATION

Propagation, in reference to plants, means multiplication or reproduction. Different plants are propagated by different methods and many may be propagated by two or more methods. The easiest and most successful methods of propagation are recommended on pages 43 through 142 along with each plants cultural requirements.

Seeds will provide the greatest quantity of plants for the least amount of time and effort. The only disadvantage to growing plants from seed is that it will take many months before the plants reach a display size.

Shallow trays, flats or even pots may be used to germinate and sprout seeds. Sow seeds in sterilized soil according to the package instructions. Cover with a pane of glass or clear sandwich wrap and keep moist until sprouts appear.

Most *ferns* may be propagated by means of spores. These are asexual reproductive organs (having neither sex) that are usually borne in brown cases on the undersides of the foliage. Spores may be germinated in either distilled water or on sterilized peat moss inside a sealed container. Keep in very low, indirect light. The rigid requirements necessary, for propagating by spores, are complicated and success is difficult for the amateur. Spores of some *ferns* may germinate as quickly as seeds and some may require as long as a year. A tiny shield like organism (prothallus) will be the first growth to appear. This growth possesses both male and female organs that unite by means of a drop of water. Fronds will appear shortly thereafter.

When the sprouts have formed true leaves, they should be transplanted to individual pots. Peat pots are made from pressed peat moss. They may be used for growing sprouts and later, planted directly into the soil. This will avoid additional transplanting shock or setbacks due to root damage.

Asplenium viviparum is commonly referred to as the *"Mother Fern."* It produces tiny plantlets right on the surface of its fronds. These plantlets may be removed along with a small portion of the leaflet and pegged down to moist peat moss.

Growth promoting hormones may be used to stimulate root growth and to increase the number of successful cuttings. They may be used with all types of cuttings except those that are rooted in water as the powder will wash off.

Leaf cuttings are those that do not include a portion of the stem. Bury $1/3$ of the leaf, tip up, in a sterilized growing medium. Keep the medium moist and provide a humid atmosphere. The new plant should appear in about eight weeks.

PROPAGATION

Stem and Leaf cuttings consist of a leaf and a portion of the stem. They can be rooted by keeping the stem moist for several weeks. This may be accomplished in a growing medium or in plain water. Plants that are rooted in plain water are less successfully transplanted into pots than those that are rooted in a medium. (Left) To start cuttings in a medium, center an unglazed, drainless clay pot inside another that is two sizes larger. Fill the cavity between the pots with the medium. Insert the stems to the base of the leaf. Fill the inner pot daily with water as the moisture will seep through the clay and into the medium. (Right) A very common method of rooting cuttings is to simply insert the stem into water. The dish shown was filled with water and covered with clear sandwich wrap. Holes were punched to insert the stems. Cuttings may be transplanted to pots after several roots appear.

Division is the fastest method of propagation for many plants. (Left) Plants that reproduce by this method are usually divided very simply by untangling the roots and cutting the plants apart. (Right) When a plant becomes as severely tangled and matted as this one, the only practical solution is to cut the root mass into halves or quarters with a serrated knife. Pot the sections individually with fresh soil and keep moist.

Allow succulent or *cactus* cuttings to dry for 1 to 7 days, depending upon size, before placing in rooting medium. The drying period will cause the cut edges to callous. This will prevent the absorption of excessive amounts of moisture that could result in rotting.

When propagating the *Piggyback plant,* remove all of the stem from a healthy leaf. Roll the leaf up, from side to side, into a funnel shape. Plant the base of the leaf $1/3$ into the soil. Cover with a clear plastic bag for high humidity.

Softwood cuttings are all cuttings that include a portion of the stem and two or more leaves. Strip the leaves from the lower 2 inches of the stem for rooting in either water or a medium. These cuttings are also commonly called "tip" or "stem" cuttings or "slips."

Begonias may be propagated by seed, division of the rhizome or by cuttings as shown. Stem and Leaf cuttings or even sections of leaves can be rooted. Regardless of the method used, cut through or sever the primary veins.

34

PROPAGATION

Soil Layering is accomplished by burying a portion of the stem in moist soil. If kept moist, roots should develop at the point of contact in a few weeks. The two plants can be cut apart at that time.

Offsets or Suckers are young plants that sporadically grow from that base or the roots of a parent plant. This method of propagation is common to *Bromeliads* and *Palms*. Depending upon the type of plant, separate from the parent by untangling the roots and cutting apart with a knife.

Runners are almost complete little plants that grow at the ends of long stems. A few house plants reproduce by this method. The *Spider plant, Strawberry begonia* and the *Zebra haworthia* are common examples. Pin the runner or baby plantlet to moist soil to grow roots before separating. Runners of the *Spider plant* will also root easily in plain water. Plantlets may be separated from the parent plant after the roots have started to form.

Cane sections can be used to propagate *Cordyline, Dieffenbachia* and most *Dracenas*. These are portions of the stem that include several sections. Plant the end or the side of the stem in a moist growing medium to root. Leaves should sprout within 1 to 2 months or shortly after roots appear.

Air Layering is a method of propagation that is used for removing bare lengths of stem from tall, leggy plants. To begin the process, cut a wedge shaped piece from the stem, just below a leaf node. The cut should be about ½ the way through.

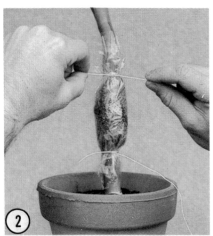

Pack moist sphagnum moss into the cut out section and around the stem. Hold in place by wrapping in clear plastic sandwich wrap. Tie the plastic in place with string just above and below the moss. Keep the moss moist.

After roots have sprouted, remove the ties and plastic wrap. Make a cut completely through the stem, just below the roots. Pot the top portion of the plant in soil. The bottom portion will sprout new foliage.

SICK PLANTS

It is often very difficult, even for experienced gardeners, to determine why a plant may be sick. Plants can experience many different kinds of illnesses and they have relatively few ways of telling us exactly what is wrong. Most plant illnesses will cause browning of the foliage. The extent of the damage and over what period of time it occurred can provide a good indication of the cause. Recent changes in location, climate or culture may also explain the problem.

This fern suffers from insufficient humidity. Browning first occurred on the edges of the leaflets where it is most susceptible to damage. The symptoms of a sunburned fern would be almost identical. If a plant is allowed to wilt, it too may demonstrate its disapproval by turning some leaves brown.

A single worm was responsible for the holes in these leaves. They, as well as slugs and snails, can cause very fast and extensive damage. Smaller insects are usually not noticed until growth becomes deformed or a few leaves become mottled with yellow.

Most tropical plants are not able to tolerate long periods of hot, direct sunlight. This palm was sunburned in a single day because it was located too near a window which received direct sunlight.

This plant had experienced no recent changes in culture. The leaves were dropping as though they were lacking in water, yet the soil was moist. A thorough inspection revealed no insects. After removing the plant from its pot, it was discovered that the roots had grown and plugged the drain hole. The rotting soil had initiated "root rot" and stopped the supply of water to the foliage.

MEALY BUGS have the appearance of tiny cotton balls. They usually locate under the leaves and in the leaf crotches. They can kill your plants if not controlled.

CONTROL: Isolate. Hand pick the pests if they are few in number. If there are many, make a 50/50 solution of rubbing alcohol and water. Apply with a cotton swab or spray.

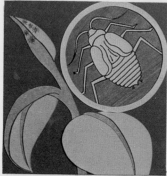

APHIDS, as most undesirable pests, suck vital plant juices. This causes poor growth or death to the plant. There are many different kinds and colors of aphids. They feed primarily on new growth.

CONTROL: Isolate. Use a systemic insecticide or spray with a mild aerosol insecticide.

RED SPIDERS are very tiny and not quickly discovered. They are found mainly on the undersides of the leaves. Yellowing leaves may be the first indication that they are present.

CONTROL: Isolate. Spray with insecticide. Repeat applications may be necessary when eggs hatch.

SCALE secrete waxy shells which they fasten to leaves and stems. They hide and lay their eggs under these shells. The scale insects are usually gray or brown. Their effects are unhealthy, stunted plants.

CONTROL: Isolate. Wash with soapy water if they are few in number or spray with an aerosol insecticide.

NATURAL HABITATS

Few plants that are available in stores have been collected, in the wild, from their natural location. All house plants however, were originally propagated from plants that did come from natural locations. These few pages have been provided to offer you a brief glimpse of how house plants grow in their natural habitats.

The lovely island of Puerto Rico has dense rain forests of luxurious growth. The annual rainfall in these areas often exceeds 200 inches. There is a natural profusion of tree ferns, epiphitical bromeliads and orchids.

The trees at an elevation of 3,000 feet are literally choked with dense growth. The island is a veritable paradise for the tropical plant enthusiast.

The beautiful island of Saint Thomas is located approximately 40 miles southeast of Puerto Rico. Bromeliads grow wild even within the capitol city of the Virgin Islands, Charlotte Amalie. Large graceful specimens precariously perch on the limbs of trees.

Tiny Tillandsias decorate the colorful Bougainvillea. Flowering Billbergia Pyramidalis grow thick along the walkways.

Many varieties of bromeliads can be found throughout Mexico. Near Ciudad Victoria, Tillandsias and orchids grow along the roadside by the thousands. Traveling south of Mexico City the foliage becomes very dense. Crotons and Cordyline grow in huge bushes while other bromeliads can be found growing on palm trees, cactus and tree limbs. One tree trunk may hold as many as 400 seedlings. The rain forests near Alzalta Falls are color-fully speckled with orchids and

thick luxurious vegetation. In the Tehuacan Desert, Tillandsias can be found growing on the shady or protected side of giant cactus. Trees laden with plants are a common sight along the Puerto Vallarta road. Some of the trees contain many different species of Tillandsia. Mexico is an ideal place to go exploring for bromeliads and the picturesque scenery is an added bonus for the plant collector.

MOTHER NATURES FAMILY ALBUM

This section is designed to familiarize you with your plant and its individual cultural requirements. All plants are listed, alphabetically, by scientific name with the exception of those that are included in the following common name groups.

AEONIUM tabulaeforme
"Saucer Plant"
Crassulaceae
Medium to high indirect sunlight. Keep the soil moist even though it is a succulent. Medium humidity. Fertilize every other month and discontinue during Winter. Propagate by seed or leaf cuttings. It is capable of growing almost two feet in diameter and the surface of the plant, is almost completely flat. Flattened leaves, perfectly arranged and nested together, form this most curious plant. Native primarily to the Canary Islands.

AESCHYNANTHUS marmoratus
"Zebra Basket Vine"
Gesneriaceae
Medium sunlight. Keep the soil moist. High humidity. Fertilize monthly and decrease to half doses during cooler months. Propagate by soft wood cuttings. An attractive trailing vine that is usually grown in a hanging container. The deep green leaves, to 4 inches long, have pale green veins. Green, tubular flowers are unspectacular. Stems are stiff and grow to about 3 feet long. Prefers fast draining soil and warm temperatures. Native to Thailand.

AESCHYNANTHUS pulcher
"Royal Red Bugler"
Gesneriaceae

Medium sunlight. Keep the soil moist. High humidity. Fertilize monthly and decrease to half doses during colder months. Propagate by soft wood cuttings. One of the heartiest varieties that is grown for both foliage and flowers. Green leaves grow to 2½ inches long. Stiff stems, to 2 feet long, hang pendulously. Long "lipstick" like tubular flowers are red and emerge from long green calyx. Allow to become dormant during colder months. Native to Java.

AGLAONEMA commutatum elegans
"Variegated Evergreen"
Araceae

Low sunlight. Allow the soil to become slightly dry between waterings. Medium humidity. Fertilize monthly with half doses. Propagate by division or soft wood cuttings. All members of this tolerant family are referred to as *"Chinese Evergreens."* Feather shaped leaves are dark green with very slight bands of grayish mottling. Tolerates insufficient sunlight, air conditioning and central heating. A slow but determined grower. Native to the Molucca Islands.

AGLAONEMA 'Fransher'
Araceae

Low sunlight. Allow the soil to become slightly dry between waterings. Medium humidity. Fertilize monthly with half doses. Propagate by division or by soft wood cuttings. A very hearty and colorful cultivar. Pointed, feather shaped leaves are colored medium green and generously variegated with grayish green. Tolerates most all adverse conditions. Pot 2 or 3 together for a very full effect or may be combined with others in a dish garden. Suitable for water culture.

ALTERNANTHERA versicolor
"Copper Leaf"
Amaranthaceae
High sunlight. Keep the soil moist. Medium humidity. Fertilize monthly. Propagate by soft wood cuttings from all growing points. Round and sharply pointed leaves are very closely set and curled. Green leaves are decorated in delicate shades of light pink and fuchsia. Abundant, almost full, sunlight is necessary to keep the foliage full. Enjoys good air circulation as do most plants. Pinch back occasionally to keep well shaped. Native to Brazil.

APHELANDRA squarrosa
"Saffron Spike"　　　'Fritz Prinsler'
Acanthaceae
Medium sunlight. Keep the soil moist. Medium, high humidity. Fertilize monthly with half doses and discontinue completely November thru February. Propagate by soft wood cuttings. An exotically colored cultivar that produces large, showy yellow bracts, usually in Summer or Autumn. Leaves, to 9 inches long, are dark green, very glossy and boldly veined with creamy yellow. In general, *Aphelandras* make poor house plants. Cultural requirements are demanding.

APHELANDRA squarrosa
"Zebra Plant"　　　'Louisae compacta'
Acanthaceae
Medium sunlight. Keep the soil moist. Medium, high humidity. Fertilize monthly with half doses and discontinue completely November thru February. Propagate by soft wood cuttings. A robust and compact variety with broad, colorful leaves. Large showy, yellow bracts form in Summer if it has been exposed to cooler temperatures in October and November. Suited best for glass house culture and not recommended for amateur gardeners.

ANTHURIUM scherzerianum
"Flamingo Flower"
Araceae
Medium, low sunlight. Keep the soil moist. High humidity. Fertilize monthly with half doses. Propagate best by division. A house plant of rather difficult culture. Unusual blooms similar to those of *Spathiphyllum*. The spathe is colored brilliant scarlet and the twisted spadix is golden yellow. They can be grown in a glass house or large terrarium. Cultivation indoors and under normal humidity is usually unsuccessful. Native to Costa Rica.

ARAUCARIA heterophylla
"Norfolk Island Pine"
Araucariaceae
Medium to high sunlight. Keep the soil moist. Medium humidity. Fertilize monthly. Propagation rather difficult by seed or cuttings. This plant is a tropical Conifer that may be grown indoors if sufficient sunlight is present. It has a pyramid shape and the tiered branches should grow in perfect arrangement. Irregular growth is indicative of insufficient sunlight. Usually a slow grower as a potted plant in the home. Originally from Norfolk Island.

ARDISIA crispa
"Coral Berry"
Myrsinaceae
Medium sunlight. Keep the soil moist. Medium humidity. Fertilize monthly and decrease to half doses in Winter. Propagate by seed or by air layering. A small tree-like plant capable of growing to 4 feet in height. Leaves, to 4 inches long, are ribbed around the edges and irregularly crimped. Flowers are followed by clusters of shiny, bright red berries that last for many months. Can be used in terrariums to add color when small.

ARDISIA polycephala
Myrsinaceae
Medium sunlight. Keep the soil moist. Medium humidity. Fertilize monthly and decrease to half doses in Winter. Propagate by seed or by air layering. A very pretty shrub-like variety with long, pointed and smooth leaves to 6 inches long. Pot 2 or 3 plants together for a full effect or pinch off terminal growth to initiate branching. Flowers are followed by red berries that blacken with age. Wilts dramatically from lack of water, but will usually recover if watered in time.

ASPIDISTRA elatior
"Cast Iron Plant"
Liliaceae
Medium to low sunlight. Keep the soil moist. Medium humidity. Fertilize monthly. Propagate by division. An enduring, lovely foliage plant that was very popular and common many years ago. So common, in fact, that many people tired of it and regarded it as undesirable. It is tolerant of low sunlight conditions and poor watering. Grows to two feet or more high. There is also a very pretty, though not as common, variegated variety. Native to China.

AZALEA (RHODODENDRON)
"Azalea"
Ericaceae
High, slightly filtered sunlight. Keep the soil moist. Use a premixed soil with a high "acid" content. Medium to high humidity with some air circulation. Fertilize half doses every 2 weeks during growth or blooming periods. Propagate by soft wood cuttings. Breathtaking clusters of vividly colored flowers. Successful indoor culture of these rather delicate plants is difficult. Usually sold as gift plants that have been "forced." Flowers hold best in a cool room.

BEAUCARNEA recurvata
"Bottle Palm" or *"Elephant Foot Tree"*
Liliaceae
High sunlight. Keep the soil moist. Medium to low humidity. Fertilize with only half doses, twice in Spring. Propagate by seed. Attractive fountains of up to four foot long leaves grow in rosette form. Foliage is similar to that of *Dracaena marginata*. Develops a very swollen, round and often misshapen, stem base. This bulbous growth is used to store a reserve supply of water for very long periods. Native primarily to Mexico.

BEGONIAS Begoniaceae

An extremely varied and huge group of plants that are grown for both foliage and flowers. There are over a thousand known species of *Begonias* and an infinite number of hybrids. They can be divided into three rough groups by their types of root systems. Fibrous, which includes *echinosepala, hispida cucullifera* the *"Piggyback Begonia"* and the common *"Wax"* or *"Bedding Begonia."* The often tall cane types also fall into this group. Rhizomatous are those with creeping rootstalks or rhizomes from which sprout both stems and roots. This group includes the bold *Rex* hybrids, *masoniana* the *"Iron Cross"* and *'Cleopatra'*. Tuberous rooted *Begonias* are grown from tubers and require a period of rest after blooms and foliage die back. These types are prized not only for their lovely foliage but for their huge, colorful and varied blooms. Generally speaking, the successful cultivation of *Begonias* in the average home is somewhat difficult. They are actually best suited as a protected patio or greenhouse plant. Many prefer moist, fresh air which is usually nonexistent indoors. Provide a filtered or indirect sunlight exposure of medium intensity. Keep the soil moist but not wet. Underwatering is preferred to overwatering as poor drainage will quickly rot their delicate root systems. Fresh air may be supplied, if necessary, by occasionally opening a nearby window. There are many varieties that can grow under normal humidity. Fertilize monthly with half doses. *Begonias* may be propagated in many ways. The leaves of the *Rex* hybrids may be cut into sections and rooted. Tips or sections of rhizomes can be rooted. Many may be reproduced by simple stem and leaf cuttings. Most all types by seed. Regardless of the method used, a humid enclosure to prevent wilting is absolutely necessary.

Begonia x 'Cleopatra'

Begonia echinosepala

Begonia hispida cucullifera

Begonia masoniana 'Iron Cross'

Begonia rex 'Her Majesty'

Begonia rex 'Merry Christmas'

Begonia x 'Edith M'

Begonia elatior

Begonia rex 'Curly Fireflush'

Begonia rex 'Green Gold'

Begonia rex 'Silver Queen'

Begonia rex 'Vesuvius'

BOWIEA volubilis
"Sea Onion" or *"Climbing Onion"*
Liliaceae
Medium sunlight. Keep the soil slightly moist. Medium humidity. Fertilize half doses monthly during growth. Propagated best by seed or by dividing offsets. This odd member of the plant kingdom is grown as a novelty rather than as a decorator plant. Six inch and larger diameter bulb annually spurts out long thin stems with peculiar, stemlike, rubbery leaves. As vine dies back, gradually withhold water until new growth appears. From South Africa.

BRASSAIA actinophylla
"Queensland umbrella tree"
Araliaceae
Medium to high sunlight. Allow the soil to become dry between waterings. Medium humidity. Prefers warm areas to 80 degrees. Fertilize monthly. Propagate by seed or half hard wood cuttings. A beautiful and lush foliage tree capable of growing to 100 feet under ideal conditions. It is a very fast grower that may require frequent rotating to keep foliage evenly shaped. Overwatering may cause dropping of older leaves. Native primarily to Australia.

BROMELIADS Bromeliaceae

Being exotic, colorful and easy to grow, *Bromeliads* are quickly becoming commonplace as house plants. Usually growing in rosette form with stiff, often arching, blade-like leaves. Scapes and flowers vary widely in most unfamiliar forms and color combinations. Some have very beautiful and smooth foliage and some have entirely gray, heavily barbed foliage. *Bromeliads* vary widely in culture as well as appearance. Some are xerophytic (grow with very little moisture). Some are epiphytic (grow on trees and other objects) as many *Orchids,* not for a source of nourishment, but as a means of support. Some are terrestrial (grow in soil) and possibly depend on it for moisture and nourishment. As a general rule, the more scale, or water absorbing gray covering that is present on the foliage, the more epiphytic or xerophytic the plant is likely to be. Most *Bromeliads* prefer medium to high filtered or indirect sunlight. Keep the soil only slightly moist and allow to become rather dry between waterings. The center "tank" formed by the leaves of many varieties should always be full with water and a mild solution of fertilizer if occasionally desired. In nature, rains are funneled by the leaves into the tank where debris, insects and bird excrement, among other things, can decay and provide nourishment. Those without a tank should be misted occasionally to supply moisture. Good, fast drainage is especially important as these plants cannot tolerate "wet feet." Propagate by offsets.

Aechmea araneosa

Aechmea X aton

Aechmea X bastantha

Aechmea X bert

Aechmea blumenavii

Aechmea caesia

Aechmea caudata variegata

Aechmea comosus pink phase

Aechmea fasciata

Aechmea fasciata var. albo-marginata

Aechmea fasciata var. variegata

Aechmea X gigant

Aechmea X Helen Miller

Aechmea mulfordii

Aechmea nudicalis X aechmea fasciata

Aechmea orlandiana var. ensign

Aechmea pectinata

Aechmea serrata

Aechmea triangularis

Ananas bracteatus

Ananas bracteatus Striatus

Ananas comosus variegatus

Billbergia pyramidalis variegata

Billbergia X fantasia

Canistrum fosterianum

Canistrum leopardinum

Guzmania lingulata major

Neoregelia carcharodon

Neoregelia carolinae tricolor selecta

Neoregelia farinosa

Neoregelia "Grande"

Neoregelia johannis

Neoregelia X luxurians

Neoregelia X promethus

Neoregelia richter hybrid

Neoregelia zonata

Quesnelia testudo

Streptocalyx floribundis

Vriesea fenestralis

Vriesea imperialis

BROMELIAD — TILLANDSIA
"Silver Birds" or "The Sky Plants"
Bromiliaceae

This is a group of mostly epiphytes and xerophytes. They are found growing in areas of both dryness, where it does not seem possible that a plant could survive, and in rain forests. Most collect, through their scaly skin, moisture out of the air. Extremely diverse and colorful blooms are characteristic. Medium to high filtered or indirect sunlight. Mist about once per week if growing in the home. Propagate by seed or offsets. Wire plant onto a piece of wood or bark for growing.

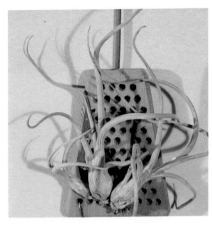

Tillandsia baileyii

Tillandsia bergeri

Tillandsia bourgaei

Tillandsia cyanea

Tillandsia festucoides

Tillandsia flexuosa

Tillandsia ionantha

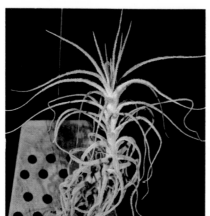

Tillandsia tectorum

Tillandsia usneoides

Tillandsia xalpa-fortin

Tillandsia xerographica

BROMELIAD—CRYPTANTHUS   Bromeliaceae
"Earth Stars"

Cryptanthus are terrestrial which means that they grow in soil and depend upon it for moisture and nutrients. They, as most *Bromeliads*, are a curious group of plants, unlike most other house plants. Varieties range in size from 2 inches to a foot and a half across. Flowers are usually white or chartreuse and rather small. Leaves are almost horizontal and close to the ground. A good plant for adding color in a terrarium. Medium, filtered sunlight. Foliage colors grow weak in insufficient sunlight. Keep the soil slightly moist and well drained. Prefers warm temperatures. Medium humidity. Fertilize half doses monthly. Propagate by seed or offsets that usually grow between the leaves instead of at the base. Removing the offsets will encourage the growth of more. Primarily from Brazil.

Cryptanthus beuckeri

Cryptanthus "It"

Cryptanthus x lubbersianus

Cryptanthus x makoyanus

CACTUS

"Succulent" is a widely used term for plants that are capable of storing water. *Cactus* have modified stems and in some cases leaves that store water. Therefore, *Cactus* are Succulents but a Succulent is not necessarily a *Cactus*. *Cactus* commonly grow spines, flowers and in some cases wool from areoles which are small, often fuzzy, growth areas that can be compared to leaf nodes on more usual plant forms. They have developed methods of protecting themselves from the hot sun such as by standing in the shadows of their ribs. Most produce exotic blooms, often much larger than themselves. It is incorrectly believed that they should be rarely watered. They are capable of surviving periods of little or no water, but are not appreciative of the situation. As a general guide, do not allow the soil to become absolutely dry. This may necessitate daily watering. During colder or Winter months, water about every 3 weeks. The soil should be kept only slightly moist, not wet.

ASTROPHYTUM myriostigma
"Bishops Cap"
Cactaceae
High sunlight. Allow the soil to become slightly dry between waterings. Medium to low humidity. Fertilize with weak solutions and only during warm months. Propagate by seed. Many *Cactus* grow in near perfect geometric shape. This five ribbed variety is completely covered with tiny gray globules. Pretty yellow flowers. Do not place in full direct sun for long periods. Plant in equal parts coarse sand, leaf mold and potting soil. Native to Mexico.

CEPHALOCEREUS senilis
"Old Man Cactus"
Cactaceae
High sunlight. Allow the soil to become slightly dry between waterings. Medium to low humidity. Fertilize with weak solutions and only during warm months. Propagate by seed. A very pretty columnar variety with fine ribs and spines. Praised for its abundant growth of pure white "hair." Capable of growing to 25 feet or higher. Reddish flowers bloom on the upper portions of the plant. Do not over or under water. Pot in fast draining mix. Native to Mexico.

FEROCACTUS
"Barrel Cactus"
Cactaceae
High sunlight. Allow the soil to become slightly dry between waterings. Medium to low humidity. Fertilize with weak solutions only during warm months. Propagate by seed. Some varieties grow to 9 feet tall and up to a foot in diameter. Grown for their colorful, up to 4 inch spines as blooming usually occurs only on older specimens. Flower colors vary in shades of white, yellow, orange and red. Native to the Southwestern United States and Mexico.

MAMMILLARIA vaupelii cristata
"Silver Brain"
Cactaceae
High sunlight. Allow the soil to become slightly dry between waterings. Medium to low humidity. Fertilize with weak solutions and only during warm months. A very popular variety of *Cactus* grown for its unusual, convoluted form. Spines are very fine. A porous, sandy soil should be used. Will not tolerate over watering. Commonly grafted onto faster growing stocks with heartier root systems. When grafting, you must use plants from the same family.

SCHLUMBERGERA bridgesii
"Christmas Cactus"
Cactaceae
Medium, high sunlight. Keep the soil slightly moist to moist. Medium humidity. Fertilize ½ doses every 2 weeks during blooming and 6 weeks after. Propagate by cuttings at joints. An epiphytic variety that should be grown in a mixture of ½ leaf mold, ¼ coarse sand and ¼ potting soil. Partially shade from sun. Provide a cooler location in Fall to start buds. Another similar variety is *S. gaertneri* the *"Easter Cactus."* Their names indicate times of blooming.

CALADIUM 'Candidum'
"White Fancy Leaved Caladium"
Araceae
Medium indirect or filtered sunlight. Keep the soil moist. Medium to high humidity. Prefers a warm location to 80 degrees. Fertilize half doses of Fish Emulsion every two weeks. Propagate by dividing the tubers. Grow in a 50/50 potting mix of Peat Moss and your regular potting soil. *Caladiums* are tuberous rooted, highly showy plants. See copy below for potting. Originally from Tropical America.

CALADIUM 'Frieda Hemple'
"Red Elephant Ear"
Araceae
Medium indirect or filtered sunlight. Keep the soil moist. Medium to high humidity. Warm area is best. Fertilize half doses of Fish Emulsion every two weeks. Propagate by dividing tubers. Start tubers in March. Plant slightly below the surface of the soil, bumpy side up. Decrease water and feeding when growth slows. When growth has stopped and you have "weaned" the soil dry, remove the tuber and store in a warm, dry location.

CALATHEA crocata
"Eternal Flame"
Marantaceae
Medium sunlight. Keep the soil moist. Medium, high humidity. Fertilize monthly and decrease to half doses October thru January. Propagate by division of the rhizome. A new, green hybrid with slightly lighter green midrib. Wavy leaves grow low and are short stemmed. Undersides are colored purple. Pot in a fast draining soil mixture and do not allow to become dry. Mist.

CALATHEA insignis
"Rattlesnake Plant"
Marantaceae
Medium sunlight. Keep the soil moist. Medium, high humidity. Fertilize monthly and decrease to half doses October thru January. Propagate by division of the rhizome. Beautifully marked foliage plant that rarely exceeds 2 feet in height when grown indoors. Long, tapering, wavy, medium green leaves are decorated with alternating sized dark spots. Undersides are purple. Do not allow to become root bound. Transplant only when necessary. Native to Brazil.

CALATHEA makoyana
"Peacock Plant"
Marantaceae
Medium sunlight. Keep the soil moist. Medium, high humidity. Fertilize monthly and decrease to half doses October thru January. Propagate by division of the rhizome. Exotically striped and blotched, glossy and leathery leaves to 9 inches long. Tall, thin stems grow from underground rhizome. There are many other commonly available and colorful varieties of *Calathea*. High humidity is preferred by most varieties, however, slightly above normal will usually satisfy.

CALCEOLARIA herbeohybrida
"Lady's Pocketbook" or *"Slipperwort"*
Scrophulariaceae
Low to medium sunlight. Keep the soil slightly moist. High humidity. Prefers cooler temperatures. Fertilize monthly. Propagate by planting seed in Spring for blooms the following year. Usually sold as a gift item in winter. Few homes are capable of fulfilling this lovely plants' growth requirements. Excellent plant for glass house culture. Warm, dry rooms can quickly diminish the tender blooms. Originally from Central America to Chile.

CARNIVOROUS PLANTS

Each is capable of ensnaring, digesting and absorbing nutrients from insects and bits of organic matter. These plants are sold as novelty items and are fascinating to watch for all ages, especially youngsters. Each plant has its own highly evolved, often elaborate, means of trapping insects. They all thrive under humid and moist growing conditions. All are ideal subjects for terrarium culture. A brandy snifter that is open at the top may also provide sufficient humidity for good growth. Do not be too generous with feedings. A small plant should only be fed one small insect at a time. Most carniverous plants are found, in nature, growing in bogs, near swamps or marshy areas. Very unusual, long stemmed blooms are characteristic of many of these plants.

DARLINGTONIA california

(carnivorous)

"Cobra Plant"
Sarraceniaceae
Medium sunlight. Keep moist with distilled water. High humidity. Pot in sandy peat moss or sphagnum. Prefers cooler locations. Propagate by division. Tall modified leaves appear very much to be a menacing nest of snakes. Insects are lured into an opening underneath the "head." The inside is a network of tiny hairs that trap the insect and eventually drown it in the reservoir below. Native to California and Oregon.

DIONAEA muscipula (carnivorous)
"Venus Fly Trap"
Droseraceae
Medium to high sunlight. Keep moist with distilled water. Medium, high humidity. Pot in chopped or shredded sphagnum moss. Prefers cooler temperatures. Propagate by leaf cuttings, seed or easiest by division of the bulbs. Traps insects in its "jaws" with incredible speed for a plant. Tiny hairs inside of the trap are the triggers. Abundant indirect sunlight is necessary for most active growth and reddish color. Native primarily to the Carolinas.

66

DROSERA spathulata (carnivorous)
"Sundew"
Droseraceae
Medium sunlight. Keep moist with distilled water. High humidity. Grows well in chopped sphagnum or sandy peat. Propagate by seed. Very tiny and most delicate carniverous plant, measuring no more than a couple of inches when mature. A minute drop of sticky, reddish fluid is secreted from each of the many hairs that grow on the foliage. They bend and push the insects onto the leaf surface where they are slowly consumed by enzymes. Native to Australia.

PINGUICULA vulgaris (carnivorous)
"Butterwort"
Lentibulariaceae
Medium sunlight. Keep moist. High humidity. Pot in sandy peat, chopped or shredded sphagnum. Propagate by seed or division. Leaves are fleshy, greasy to the touch and curled at the edges. Insects are lured onto the foliage by their covering of digestive fluids. They move about freely at first and are slowly overcome and absorbed by the leaves of the plant. *P. luteola* is similar with yellow flowers. Native to Mexico.

SARRACENIA purpurea (carnivorous)
"Pitcher Plant"
Sarraceniaceae
Medium sunlight. Keep moist with distilled water. High humidity. Pot in sandy peat or sphagnum. Propagate by division. Attractively colored foliage lures insects. The modified leaves hold water and are covered inside with hairs that grow downward to discourage escape. Once in the water, the insects are drowned and digested. Its natural habitat ranges from the Carolinas to Labrador.

CEROPEGIA woodii *"Rosary Vine"* Asclepiadaceae (below, right)
Medium sunlight. Allow the soil to become slightly dry between waterings. Medium humidity. Fertilize monthly. Propagate by softwood cuttings, soil layering or by division. Attractively marbled and paired leaves usually grow no larger than ¾". Pretty, purple, lantern shaped flowers. **CEROPEGIA debilis** *"Needle Vine"* (below, left) Unusual, tangled, thin leaved vine. Provide same culture as for *C. woodii.*

CHLOROPHYTUM comosum (below, left)
CHLOROPHYTUM comosum 'Vittatum' (below, right)
"Spider Plants" or *"Airplane Plants"* Liliaceae
Medium sunlight. Keep the soil moist. Medium humidity. Fertilize monthly. Propagate by division or by rooting plantlets. Attractive, dense clumps of narrow, curving leaf blades. Plantlets grow on stems that hang well below the pot. They also have vigorously growing, bulbous roots.

CISSUS antarctica
"Kangaroo Ivy"
Vitaceae
Medium to high sunlight. Allow the soil to become slightly dry between waterings. Medium humidity. Fertilize monthly. Propagate by soft wood cuttings. With abundant sunlight, this is a fast grower. A large, pendulous vine that will climb with tendrils or hang attractively below a pot. The shiny, toothed leaves grow 2 to 3 inches long on stems to 8 feet. Pinching off the terminal growth will keep the foliage full and compact. Originated from Australia.

CISSUS capensis
"Indoor Grape"
Vitaceae
Medium sunlight. Allow the soil to become slightly dry between waterings. Medium humidity. Fertilize monthly. Propagate by soft wood cuttings. A very nice variety, much resembling the true *"Grape."* Leaves are fresh green, thin and very broad to 5 inches. Climbs by tendrils or will hang far below the pot. Keep away from very hot sunlight. It may be allowed to grow very long if desired or pinch back occasionally to keep full near pot.

CISSUS discolor
"Begonia Treebine"
Vitaceae
Medium sunlight. Keep the soil moist. Medium, high humidity. Fertilize half doses monthly. Propagate by soft wood cuttings. Beautifully painted, soft leaves to 5 inches long are colored moss green and silver gray. The undersides of the leaves and the stems are maroon. Tendril climbing if trained, or will hang below the container if desired. More particular about care than other varieties. It will not tolerate a room with low humidity.

CISSUS rhombifolia
"Grape Ivy"
Vitaceae
Medium sunlight. Allow the soil to become slightly dry between waterings. Medium humidity. Fertilize monthly. Propagate best by soft wood cuttings. This variety of *Cissus* is very popular as a house plant. It has luxurious foliage that can be trained or allowed to hang. The leaflets grow to 4" long on stems usually no longer than 10 feet. Occasionally pinch off terminal growth for full and branching foliage. Attractive to Red Spider. Native to South America.

CISSUS rotundifolia
"Arabian Wax Cissus"
Vitaceae
Medium sunlight. Allow the soil to become slightly dry between waterings. Medium humidity. Fertilize monthly. Propagate by soft wood cuttings. Almost completely round leaves are medium green and glossy with fine teeth. Grows quickly with relatively easy care. It is tolerant of the forgetful waterer. Climbs, as do other *Cissus,* by tendrils or becomes pendant with the weight of the foliage. Usually does not require pinching.

CISSUS striata
"Miniature Grape Ivy"
Vitaceae
Medium sunlight. Keep the soil moist. Medium humidity. Fertilize monthly. Propagate by soft wood cuttings. A small vine with compound, to 2 inches wide, 5 leaflet foliage. The leaves are dark green and have lighter green midribs. Stems are reddish. Tends to become more pendulous than climbing. Not widely available in all nurseries as it is rather small and slow growing. Native to South America.

CODIAEUM

"Crotons"

Euphorbiaceae

High indirect sunlight. Allow the soil to become slightly dry between waterings. High humidity. Only during warm months, fertilize with half doses. Propagate by seed, soft wood cuttings in Spring or by air layering. Extremely colorful plants, some of which are capable of growing each leaf a different shade or even color. The leathery leaves of these small shrubs vary widely in shape. If new leaves are mostly green, this is a sign of insufficient sunlight.

Codiaeum appendiculatum

Codiaeum 'Aucubaefolium'

Codiaeum 'Imperialis'

Codiaeum 'Norwood Beauty'

Codiaeum 'Punctatum aureum'

71

COLEUS Labiatae

High indirect sunlight. Keep the soil moist. Medium humidity. Fertilize half doses twice monthly. Propagate by seed or by soft wood cuttings under a humid enclosure. Fast growing pot plants to 2 feet high with beautifully colored leaves to 4 inches long. All varieties shown have upright growth habit except *'Trailing Queen'*. They enjoy warm rooms and much water. Do not allow soil to become completely dry as the plant may drop lower leaves. Pinch to keep full and branching. Remove superfluous blooms. Good for water culture.

Coleus blumei 'Frilled Fantasy'

Coleus blumei 'Golden Bedder'

Coleus blumei 'The Chief'

Coleus blumei 'Victoria'

Coleus rehneltianus 'Trailing Queen'

COLUMNEA gloriosa
Gesneraceae
Medium sunlight. Keep the soil moist. High humidity. Fertilize monthly and decrease to half doses July thru October. Propagate best by soft wood cuttings. A long stemmed trailing plant that is cultivated for both foliage and unusual tubular blooms that are most abundant January thru April. Leaves, to 1 inch long, are covered with fine hairs. This particular variety prefers humid, glass house culture but there are many others that will thrive in the average home.

CORDYLINE terminalis 'Baby Ti'
"Ti Plant" or "Hawaiian Ti"
Liliaceae
Medium sunlight. Keep the soil moist. Medium, high humidity. Fertilize monthly. Propagate by air layering, offsets or by rooting sections of the cane. The smallest and most popular variety. Capable of growing to 3 feet in height. Leaves grow to 6 inches in length on short stems. They are dark green with magenta colored streaks, primarily in the margins. Becomes rather dormant and unproductive during Summer. Native to Hawaii.

CRASSULA argentea
(bot. C. arborescens)
"Jade plant"
Crassulaceae
High sunlight. Allow the soil to become slightly dry between waterings. Low to medium humidity. Fertilize monthly. Propagate by leaf cuttings or best by soft wood cuttings in sandy soil. Stems will also root in water. This almost indestructable plant derives its name from its lovely foliage color. It develops a thick, juicy trunk. Moving outdoors occasionally for additional sunlight is certain to be beneficial.

CTENANTHE oppenheimana tricolor
"Never Never Plant"
Marantaceae
Medium sunlight. Keep the soil moist. Medium, high humidity. Fertilize monthly. Propagate by division of older plants. There are several varieties of these colorful foliage plants. Very similar in growth to *Maranta*. Two tone green leaves, to 1 foot long, are irregularly splashed with cream. Undersides are maroon. Place pot on a tray of pebbles with water or mix with other plants for added humidity. Native to Brazil.

CYCLAMEN persicum
"Florists Cyclamen"
Primulaceae
Medium to high indirect sunlight. Keep the soil moist. Medium humidity, however, some varieties require high humidity. Fertilize ½ doses fish emulsion twice per month. Grow from tubers. Prized for their lovely flag-like blooms. Start tubers in June when they are dormant. Pot the tuber half into the surface of the soil. Use a 50/50 soil mixture of peat moss and regular potting mix. Decrease watering and feeding as dormancy begins.

CYMBALARIA muralis
"Kenilworth Ivy" or *"Ivy Geranium"*
Scrophulariaceae
Medium sunlight. Keep the soil moist. Medium, high humidity. Fertilize monthly. Propagate by seed, soil layering or by soft wood cuttings under a humid enclosure. Division of older plants can also be used but is often damaging to the tender stems. A very pretty hanging vine with abundant, white or bluish flowers. Soft, fresh green, almost round and lobed leaves to 1 inch wide. Usually grown in a hanging container. Suffers in warm or dry rooms.

DIEFFENBACHIA *"Dumb Canes"* Araceae

Exotic foliage plants of interesting form. Their variously shaded, green leaves are usually splashed or mottled with white, cream or yellow coloring. They become tall and palm like after many years of growth. Eventually develops a thick juicy trunk that will require staking. Calcium oxalate crystals, contained in the stems and leaves, can cause swelling and severe pain if touched to the skin. If a *Dieffenbachia* is bitten or taken internally, illness will surely result along with a temporary loss of speech, thus the name *"Dumb Cane"* is derived. Branches of new foliage will sprout from the sides of the cane if the entire top is cut off. The top may be rooted in plain water. Overwatering or poor drainage may be disastrous. Provide Medium sunlight. Allow the soil to become slightly dry between waterings. Medium humidity is required for the varieties shown below. Fertilize monthly with half doses. Propagate by joint cuttings or safest by air layering.

Dieffenbachia amoena

Dieffenbachia oerstedii variegata

Dieffenbachia picta 'Rud. Roehrs'

Dieffenbachia picta 'Superba'

DIOSCOREA elephantopus
"Tortoise Plant" or "Hottentot Bread"
Dioscoreaceae
Medium sunlight. Keep the soil moist. Medium, high humidity. Fertilize monthly when productive and showing new growth. Propagate by dividing the tuber. Unique, deciduous plant, usually grown as a novelty. Develops a monstrous, deeply corrugated, above ground tuber that grows to 3 feet in diameter when mature. One or more branched vines emerge from the tuber each year. Leaves are thin and heart shaped to 4 inches long.

DIZYGOTHECA elegantissima
"Aralia, False Threadleaf"
Araliaceae
Medium sunlight. Keep the soil slightly moist. Prefers warm temperatures to 80 degrees. Medium humidity. Fertilize monthly. Propagate by seed or air layering. This is a tree-like shrub that is capable of growing to a height of 5 feet or more. They are usually planted 2 or 3 to a pot for a bushier appearance. Overwatering or poor drainage can easily cause this plant to lose its lower leaves. The *"False Aralia"* originally came from New Hebrides in the Coral Sea.

DORSTENIA contrajerva
"Inside Out Fig"
Moraceae
Medium sunlight. Keep the soil moist. Medium, high humidity. Fertilize monthly. Propagate by seed or by division of the rootstalk. Slightly quilted and very shiny leaves to 8 inches long. Unisexual flowers are borne in the surface of flattened or irregularly shaped, cup-like recepticles. To obtain seed, enclose "flower" with a small paper bag and secure in place with string until ripened. Best grown in a warm and shady glass house. Tropical America.

DRACAENAS Liliaceae

"Dragon Lilies"

Dramatic and often artistic decorator plants. Most are tall growing with fountains of arching, blade like leaves at the tops of their naked, cane like stems. They are very tolerant of indoor conditions, including insufficient sunlight. For optimum growth, provide medium sunlight. Keep the soil moist. Medium humidity. Fertilize monthly. Varieties *D. sanderiana* and *godseffiana* are small and suitable for growing in terrariums or dish gardens. *D. marginata* and the gaily colored *'Tricolor'* have thin leaf blades, to 18 inches long, that grow on twisted, to 10 foot, stems. The robust and luxurious *D. fragrans* varieties are capable of growing as high as 20 feet. Its ribbony, leaf blades are very broad and can exceed 2 feet in length. Propagate by soft wood cuttings, air layering or by rooting sections of the stems.

Dracaena draco

Dracaena fragrans massangeana

Dracaena marginata

Dracaena marginata 'Tricolor'

Dracaena craigii 'Compacta'

Dracaena deremenis 'Bausei'

Dracaena fragrans 'Victoriae'

Dracaena godseffiana

Dracaena sanderiana

Dracaena sanderiana 'Borinquensis'

ECHEVERIA
Crassulaceae
High sunlight. Allow the soil to become slightly dry between waterings. Medium humidity. Fertilize half doses monthly and discontinue completely during winter. Propagate by seed, leaf cuttings or by offsets. Small, succulent rosettes that are suitable for growing indoors, in warm, sunny windows. Leaves are waxy in appearance and are often covered with a gray or bluish powder. Allow to go into dormancy during Winter by relocating in a cooler area with less water. Native to Mexico.

EPISCIA cupreata 'Acajou'
Gesneraceae
Medium sunlight. Keep the soil moist. Medium humidity. Fertilize half doses, twice monthly. Propagate by leaf and stem cuttings or by runners. *Episcas* are commonly referred to as the *"Flame Violets."* Leaves, to 4 inches long, are pearlized, light green with dark, reddish brown coloring in the margin between the veins. 5 lobed, reddish orange, tubular flowers bloom the year round, but most vigorously, March thru August.

EPISCIA dianthiflora
"Lace flower vine"
Gesneriaceae
Medium sunlight. Keep the soil moist but not wet. Near high humidity. Fertilize monthly. Propagate by leaf-stem cuttings or by rooting runners in soil. Vigorously sends out runners with evenly spaced plantlets. Enjoys house temperatures but will wither away with insufficient humidity. Exotically frilled, delicate white flowers. Thrives in terrariums. Native of Mexico.

EUPHORBIA pulcherrima
'Eckespoint'
"Poinsettia" or "Christmas Star"
Euphorbiaceae

High sunlight. Keep the soil moist. Fertilize monthly. Propagate by soft or hard wood cuttings. A showy hybrid with beautiful red bracts and usually sold as a gift item at Christmas time. Requires cutting back and a rest period before blooming again. A lovely white hybrid is also available during the holiday season. Grows into a large shrub if planted outdoors in an almost full sun location.

FATSHEDERA lizei
"Botanical Wonder"
Araliaceae

Medium sunlight. Keep the soil moist. Medium humidity. Prefers cooler temperatures up to 65 degrees. Fertilize monthly. Propagate by soft wood cuttings. A hybrid between the *"Japanese Aralia"* and *"Irish Ivy"*. Has good qualities from both. Pinch back terminal growth to initiate branching if necessary. Usually requires support. The variegated variety has white colorings in the leaf margins but is somewhat more difficult to grow.

FENESTRARIA
"Baby Toes"
Aizoaceae

High sunlight. Keep the soil only slightly moist and almost no water during Winter. Low to medium humidity. Fertilize with ¼ doses only during warm months. A small succulent that is grown for its unusual form. Found in nature with its tiny 1½ inch leaves almost completely buried in sand. It uniquely absorbs sunlight through the leaf center. A translucent lens at the end of each leaf regulates the amount of light that enters. Native to Africa.

FERNS and FERN-LIKE PLANTS

The old-fashioned *"Boston Fern"* continues to hold one of the most prominent positions among house plants. Many beautiful varieties of ferns will easily grow in conditions existing in the average home. When purchasing a fern that has been growing or displayed in an area of high humidity, it is wise to "harden" the foliage. This is done by placing a clear, lightweight plastic bag completely over the plant to duplicate the humidity in which it was cultivated. Over a period of one to two weeks, from the bottom, cut away equal portions of the bag. Each day, further acclimating the plant to the humidity of its new home. Ferns, in general, are shade loving plants that thrive under humid conditions. They are non-flowering and reproduce by means of spores. These are asexual reproductive organs (having neither sex) that are usually borne in brown cases on the undersides of the foliage. Their leaves are referred to as "fronds."

ADIANTUM hispidulum
"Australian Maidenhair"
Filices
Low sunlight. Keep the soil moist. High humidity. Fertilize monthly and decrease to half doses during Winter. Propagate best by division. Thin, upright stems are branched into 3 to 7 fingers. Leaflets, to ¾ inch, are fresh green and overlapping. Care must be taken with all *"Maidenhairs"* to provide excellent drainage and to keep the soil moist. On mature plants, the appearance of an occasional dying frond is the natural process of providing room for new growth.

ADIANTUM raddianum (A. cuneatum)
"Delta Maidenhair"
Filices
Medium sunlight. Keep the soil moist. Medium to high humidity. Fertilize monthly and decrease to half doses during Winter. Propagate best by division. Among the laciest and heartiest of the *"Maidenhairs."* Tiny, fan like leaflets, to ⅜ inch wide, are loosely spaced on thin, wiry stems. Overall effect is billowy and cloud like. Variety most compatable to indoor culture. Often grows well in kitchen or bathroom where humidity is highest. Native to Brazil.

ADIANTUM raddianum 'Pacific Maid'
"Pacific Maid"
Filices

Low sunlight. Keep the soil moist. High humidity. Fertilize monthly and decrease to half doses during Winter. Propagate best by division. One of the loveliest and most commonly available varieties. Fan shaped leaflets grow to ¾ inches wide. They are overlapping and densely set on thin, black stems. Growth is very full. Cultivation indoors is usually unsuccessful unless provisions are made for additional humidity. Keep out of cold drafts.

ADIANTUM trapeziforme
"Giant Maidenhair"
Filices

Low sunlight. Keep the soil moist. High humidity. Fertilize monthly and decrease to half doses during Winter. Propagate best by division. A large variety with, to 1½ inch long, almost trapezoid shaped leaflets that are finely and irregularly lobed. The almost pinkish color of new growth quickly turns bright green. Prefers warm temperatures between 65 and 75 degrees. Suitable for glass house culture or growing in terrariums. Native primarily to Central and South America.

ASPARAGUS asparagoides
                              myrtifolius
"Baby Smilax"
Liliaceae

Medium sunlight. Allow the soil to become slightly dry between waterings. Medium to high humidity. Fertilize monthly. Propagate by seed or by division. Commonly grown for use with flower arrangements. Will cascade over the sides of a container or may be trained on strings. Tiny leaves, to ½ inch, are shiny, stiff and pointed. Thin stems are wiry and become very tangled. Native to South America.

ASPARAGUS densiflorus 'Meyeri'
"Plume Asparagus"
Liliaceae
Medium to high sunlight. Keep the soil moist. Medium humidity. Fertilize monthly. Propagate by seed or division. Stiff, upright stems, to 2 feet, are thickly dressed with tiny branches of flattened, green stems. Both this variety and the *"Sprengeri Fern"* have thick, bulb like roots and can become pot bound very quickly. A true friend to the forgetful waterer. Tolerates adverse conditions.

ASPARAGUS densiflorus 'Sprengeri'
"Sprengeri Fern"
Liliaceae
High sunlight. Keep the soil moist. Medium humidity. Fertilize monthly. Propagate by seed or division. The stiff, arching stems of this durable fern like plant grow to 4 feet long. They are delicately furnished with flattened, green stems. Tiny, white flowers are followed by the growth of colorful red berries. A very fast grower under favorable conditions. Most commonly grown in hanging containers. Native to South Africa.

ASPARAGUS setaceus
"Plumosa Fern" or "Asparagus Fern"
Liliaceae
Medium to high sunlight. Allow the soil to become slightly dry between waterings. Medium humidity. Fertilize monthly. Propagate by seed or division. The laciest and most fern-like variety of Asparagus. Sends up long and branched stems that are fully clothed with tiny needle shaped stems that are arranged on a flat plane. The stems, when new and flexible, may be staked or trained to twine up a pot hanger. The stems are also very distantly set with thorns.

ASPARAGUS retrofractus
"Zig Zag Fern"
Liliaceae
High sunlight. Keep the soil moist. Medium humidity. Fertilize monthly and decrease to half doses in Winter. Propagate by seed. Long firm stems sprout plumes of thin branches densely clothed in soft needle-like leaves. Abundant sunlight is necessary to keep growth vigorous. Develops a large and very powerful root system in a relatively short period of time.

ASPLENIUM mayii
Filices
Low to medium sunlight. Keep the soil moist and well drained. Medium, high humidity. Fertilize monthly. Propagate by spores. Flexible, arching fronds are medium green with a slight cast of purple. The soft green leaflets are irregularly cut and lobed. A *"Spleenwort"* as other members of the *Asplenium* family. At one time, thought to be a remedy for disorders of the spleen.

ASPLENIUM nidus
"Birdsnest Fern"
Filices
Low to medium sunlight. Keep the soil moist. Medium humidity. Fertilize monthly. Propagate by spores. A popular variety that tolerates moderate indoor conditions. Fronds on older plants can grow to 3 feet long. New fronds are often very wavy or irregularly shaped. Avoid very cold temperatures or cold drafts. Turn pot frequently to keep foliage well shaped. This plant originated from a triangular shaped area bordered by Australia, Japan and India.

ASPLENIUM squamulatum
Filices
Low to medium sunlight. Keep the soil moist. Medium, high humidity. Fertilize monthly. Propagate by spores which are borne on the undersides of the fronds. A lovely little fern with leathery fronds radiating outward to over 1 foot when mature. Narrower fronds and less undulating than the *"Birdsnest Fern."* Prefers temperatures between 65 and 75 degrees. Pot in a mixture of 2 parts potting soil and 1 part peat moss or finely chopped sphagnum.

ASPLENIUM viviparum
"Mother Fern"
Filices
Medium sunlight. Keep the soil moist. Medium to high humidity. Fertilize monthly. Propagate by rooting plantlets. Uniquely, it produces young plantlets right on the surface of its fronds. When the plantlets have grown a couple of leaves, they with a small amount of the frond can be rooted in soil under a moist atmosphere. Not extremely tolerant of dry heated rooms. Native to islands in the West Indian Ocean.

BUGULA species
"Air Fern"
This is a fern-like growth that requires no watering or feeding. It was once believed to be a plant but is actually a very low form of animal life. It is sold through nurseries and mail order houses as a novelty. In true form, it is actually brownish in color but for appearances, it is commonly dyed green. It also produces a slight but rather disagreeable odor. Originally from the French and English coastal areas.

CYRTOMIUM falcatum
"Holly Fern"　　　　**'Rochefordianum'**
Filices

Low to medium sunlight. Keep the soil moist. Medium humidity. Fertilize monthly. Propagate by spores or by dividing the rhizome. Shiny, leathery, dark green leaflets have toothed edges. Slightly hairy stalks grow in compact clusters to 18 inches. *C. falcatum,* also a *"Holly Fern,"* has more distantly spaced leaflets with smooth edges and stalks that grow to 2 feet. These are very durable ferns that will continue to grow even under adverse conditions.

DAVALLIA fejeensis
"Rabbits Foot Fern"
Filices

Medium sunlight. Keep the soil moist. Medium to high humidity. Fertilize monthly. Propagate by dividing and rooting the rhizomes. This lacy fern grows epiphitically with hairy rhizomes that creep over the soil or sphagnum. They are usually planted in mossed baskets so that they can spread and grow into a ball of foliage. There are several varieties of this unique plant, most requiring the same culture. Found in Australia where they grow on rocks and trees.

NEPHROLEPIS exaltata bostoniensis
"Boston Fern"
Filices

Medium sunlight. Keep the soil moist. Medium, high humidity. Fertilize monthly and discontinue in Winter. Propagate easily by division. Very popular in the Twenties and is presently enjoying a comeback. The fronds can grow in excess of 4 feet when mature. Enjoys being somewhat pot bound until growth slows. Foliage may turn brown if exposed to direct sunlight, central heating drafts or very dry air. This variety of *Nephrolepis* was discovered in Boston.

NEPHROLEPIS ex. bostoniensis compacta
"Dwarf Boston Fern"
Filices
Medium sunlight. Keep the soil moist. Medium, high humidity. Fertilize monthly, and discontinue during Winter. Propagate by division. Culture is the same as for the *"Boston Fern."* Fronds grow to 18 inches in length and are more upright than the larger variety. *Nephrolepis* experience their fastest and most vigorous growth during warm seasons and when slightly pot bound.

NEPHROLEPIS ex. 'Fluffy Ruffles'
"Fluffy Ruffle Fern"
Filices
Medium sunlight. Keep the soil moist. Medium to high humidity. Fertilize monthly and discontinue during Winter. Propagate by division. Short fronds to 1 foot in length are densely set with finely divided and ruffled leaflets. They are stiff, upright and compact as the *"Irish Lace Fern"* yet not quite as dense and divided. Enjoys some air circulation and will tolerate a near medium humidity.

NEPHROLEPIS exaltata 'Norwoodii'
"Irish Lace Fern"
Filices
Medium sunlight. Keep the soil moist. Medium to high humidity. Fertilize monthly and discontinue during Winter. Propagate by division. Very short, wide and highly divided fronds grow to about 1 foot in length. It has upright and compact growth habits, becoming full with overlapping foliage when mature. Do not mist. Enjoys warm temperatures. Provide higher humidity if leaflets begin to turn brown.

NEPHROLEPIS ex. 'Rooseveltii plumosa'
"Roosevelt Fern" or "Tall Feather Fern"
Filices

Medium sunlight. Keep the soil moist. Medium to high humidity. Fertilize monthly and discontinue during Winter. Propagate by division. A fast growing variety running only second in popularity to the *"Boston Fern."* The fronds grow to 3 feet in length and the leaflets are rippled and undulate. Allow to become somewhat pot bound until growth slows. Enjoys air circulation. Keep away from central heating drafts.

NEPHROLEPIS exaltata 'Whitmanii'
"Whitman Fern" or "Feather Fern"
Filices

Medium sunlight. Keep the soil moist. Medium to high humidity. Fertilize monthly and discontinue during Winter. Propagate by division. As indicated by its name, this variety is leathery and open in appearance. The fronds can grow to 2 feet in length. Keep out of hot direct sunlight and drafts. Allow to become slightly pot bound until growth slows. Pot all *Nephrolepis* in moisture retaining soil mixtures containing $1/3$ peat moss or chopped sphagnum.

PELLAEA falcata
Filices

Medium sunlight. Keep the soil moist. Medium humidity. Fertilize monthly. Propagate by spores. Glossy, leathery leaflets are long and slightly pointed. Fronds eventually grow low to the ground and vary in length from 10 to 15 inches when mature. Stalks are brown and hairy. May be potted singly or may be grouped with others for unusual texture. Suffers in warm rooms. Fronds that grow small could be an indication of insufficient sunlight or fertilizer. Native to Australia and New Zealand.

PELLAEA rotundifolia
"Button fern" or "Roundleaf fern"
Filices

Medium sunlight. Keep the soil moist. Medium humidity. Prefers warm temperatures. Fertilize monthly. Propagate by spores. A small fern with arching, low and to a foot long fronds consisting of ¾ inch diameter round and leathery leaflets. Good for adding texture to a mass planting or as an individual pot plant. They are also nice plants for large terrariums. Originally from New Zealand.

PELLAEA viridis
"Green Cliff Brake"
Filices

Medium sunlight. Keep the soil moist. Medium humidity. Fertilize monthly. Propagate by spores. An easy to grow variety for a cool room. Medium green fronds grow to 2 feet in length and darken in color when mature. The stalks are evenly spaced with leaflets that are single at the end of the frond and become divided into many segments toward the base. Native primarily to South Africa.

PHYLLITIS scolopendrium
"Hart's Tongue Fern"
Filices

Medium sunlight. Keep the soil moist. Medium humidity. Fertilize monthly. Propagate by spores. A very beautiful light green fern, of easy culture, with gracefully arching blade-like fronds to over a foot in length. They are lobed at the base and rippled or wavy near the edges. Locate in a cool room for optimum growth. Rotate the pot occasionally as the fronds will grow toward the light source, causing the plant to become lopsided. Enjoys misting.

PHYLLITIS scolopendrium 'Crispifolium'
Polypodiaceae
Medium sunlight. Keep the soil moist. Medium to high humidity. Prefers cooler temperatures. Fertilize monthly. Propagate by spores. Long narrow, dark green fronds with very wavy or rippled margins are characteristic. Not especially prized for the lushness of its foliage, but for its unique form. *Phyllitis scolopendrium 'Crispum'* or *"Crisped Hart's Tongue"* is another, more popular variety that is very similar yet has wider fronds.

PLATYCERIUM
"Staghorn Ferns" or "Elkhorn Ferns"
Filices
Medium sunlight. Keep the moss or soil moist. Most prefer high humidity. Ask your local nurseryman about your particular variety. Fertilize monthly with half doses. Propagate by offsets at base. There are many varieties of these unusual ferns. Frond shapes and sizes vary from 8 inch forked antlers to 8 foot elephant ears. Commonly grown in sphagnum moss or in mossed baskets. Dip to water. Fresh air circulation is necessary for optimum growth.

POLYPODIUM aureum 'Mandianum'
"Crisped Blue Fern" or "Lettuce Fern"
Filices
Low to medium sunlight. Keep the soil moist. Medium humidity. Fertilize monthly and decrease to half doses during Winter. Propagate by division of the rhizome. A striking fern variety having upright fronds that droop from the weight of their foliage. The wide blades are deeply cut and "shredded" near the tips. Keep away from direct sunlight. Variety *P. aureum 'Undulatum'* the *"Blue Fern"* is very similar except the deeply cut fronds have smoother edges.

POLYPODIUM piloselloides
Filices

Medium sunlight. Keep the soil moist. Medium to high humidity. Fertilize monthly and decrease to half doses in Winter. Propagate by spores or by division of the rhizome which is a creeping rootstock above or below the ground that produces roots and leaves or fronds. Small dark green fronds, to 4 inches long. Often grown in mossed baskets which allow the plant to creep and root freely. Locate in a warm room and out of direct sunlight.

POLYSTICHUM setosum
"Bristle Fern"
Filices

Medium indirect sunlight. Keep the soil moist. Medium to high humidity. Fertilize half doses monthly and discontinue during Winter. Propagate by spores or by dividing the rhizome. Fresh green fronds, to 1 foot long, are generously furnished with feathery, irregularly lobed leaflets. Prefers room temperatures between 65 and 75 degrees. Fronds wilt and turn brown very quickly if soil is allowed to become excessively dry. Originally from Japan.

PTERIS cretica 'Childsii'
"Child's Cretan Brake Fern"
Filices

Medium sunlight. Keep the soil moist. Medium, high humidity. Fertilize monthly and decrease to half doses in Winter. Propagate by spores. Fresh green leaflets are divided at tips on mature fronds. The leaves are rippled with finely ruffled edges. Fronds grow to 2 feet long. Very fast growing under proper conditions. Good subject for terrariums when young.

PTERIS multifida
"Chinese Brake" or "Spider Brake Fern"
Filices
Low to medium sunlight. Keep the soil moist. Medium humidity. Fertilize monthly and decrease to half doses in Winter. Propagate by spores. Long, thin, dark green leaflets are widely spaced on stalks. A hearty variety that has been commonly used as an indoor plant for many years. Tolerates rather low sunlight conditions and does not easily damage from insufficient watering.

PTERIS quadriaurita 'Argyraea'
"Silver Bracken"
Filices
Medium sunlight. Keep the soil moist. Medium, high humidity. Fertilize monthly and decrease to half doses in Winter. Propagate by spores. A favorite of the table ferns for its large divided leaflets which are colored light gray in the center. Fronds can grow to 4 feet under proper conditions and when mature. Excellent for adding color to terrariums. Repot all *Pteris ferns* before they become pot bound. Native to India.

PTERIS vittata
Filices
Medium sunlight. Keep the soil moist. Medium, high humidity. Fertilize monthly and decrease to half doses in Winter. Propagate by spores. Prefers warm rooms but keep out of central heating drafts. Narrow leaflets are dark green, glossy and leathery in appearance. They are closely arranged on arching stalks to 2 feet long. Leaf edges are finely toothed. Enjoys misting. Very tolerant of abuse in relation to other ferns.

SELAGINELLA kraussiana brownii
"Cushion moss" or "Club moss"
Selaginellaceae
Low indirect sunlight. Keep the soil well drained and moist. High humidity. Fertilize monthly with weak solutions. Propagate by division or by rooting tiny branches in moist peat. Somewhat difficult to grow in the average home yet thrives in terrariums. Grows in a nicely shaped, full mound and supports itself on thin aerial roots. Direct sunlight can be very harmful to this delicate plant. Native to the Azores, a group of islands centered in the North Atlantic Ocean.

SELAGINELLA lepidophylla
"Resurrection Plant"
Selaginellaceae
Medium sunlight. Keep the soil moist. Medium to high humidity. Fertilize half doses monthly. Propagate by offsets. An unusual fern like plant that is sold as a novelty. It curls its fronds into a tight clump when dry. After being watered, it will unfold completely and show fresh green coloring irregardless of how long it has been dry. Grows to 4 or 5 inches in diameter. Native to Texas.

SELAGINELLA uncinata
"Rainbow Fern" or "Peacock Fern"
Selaginellaceae
Low sunlight. Keep the soil moist. Medium, high humidity. Fertilize half doses monthly. Propagate by division or by rooting joint cuttings. Faintly cast with peacock blue coloring. A beautiful plant to spill over the sides of a hanging container or to use as a spreading ground cover in terrariums. Grows several inches thick in a humid environment. Must be grown in a warm, shady location. *S. kraussiana,* a similar variety has yellowish green coloring.

FICUS Moraceae
"Rubber Plants" or "Ornamental Figs"
Very desirable and readily available group of evergreen and deciduous plants. The plants described in this section, however, are all evergreen which means year round enjoyment. Grown for their luxuriant and varied foliage. They are strong, vigorous growers even when young. Related to the true *Fig* tree. Practically all varieties of *Ficus* thrive indoors and are tolerant of poor light, watering and humid conditions that may exist.

FICUS benjamina
"Weeping Fig"
Moraceae
Medium to high sunlight. Allow to become rather dry between waterings. Medium to high humidity. Prefers warm temperatures. Fertilize monthly. Propagate by· air layering. A very desirable decorator tree with a clean, narrow trunk and small, to three inch, glossy green leaves. Abundant sunlight is necessary to keep the foliage full. Often drops leaves when moved to a new environment or location. Can exceed 25 feet in height. Originally from India.

FICUS diversifolia
"Mistletoe ficus"
Moraceae
Medium to high sunlight. Allow the soil to become slightly dry between waterings. Medium humidity. Prefers warm temperatures to 75 degrees. Fertilize monthly. Propagate by air layering. A small, round leaved tree, growing to three feet or more in height. Brown spots on foliage are characteristic. Almost continuously produces small inedible fruit. A slow growing but delightful shrub for indoor culture. Originally from Malaya.

FICUS elastica 'Decora'
"Rubber Plant"
Moraceae
High sunlight. Allow the soil to become slightly dry between waterings. Low to medium humidity. Fertilize monthly. Propagate by air-layering. Tolerant of abuse, fast growing and usually inexpensive for its size. It is actually a tree that is capable of growing to immense proportions under ideal conditions. It prefers as much sunlight as possible but will handle most indoor conditions. Originally from India.

FICUS elastica 'Decora Schrijvereana'
Moraceae
Medium to high sunlight. Allow the soil to become slightly dry between waterings. Medium humidity. Fertilize monthly. Propagate best by air layering. Beautiful cultivar with broad leaves to 1 foot long. Subtly colored with small, irregular splashes of dark foam green on a fresh green background. Adapts very well to indoor culture. Pinch back terminal growth to initiate branching.

FICUS elastica variegata
"Variegated Rubber Plant"
Moraceae
Medium to high sunlight. Allow the soil to become slightly dry between waterings. Medium humidity. Fertilize monthly. Propagate best by air layering. A variegated form of *Ficus elastica*. Capable of growing to immense proportions. Leaves, to 1 foot long, are colored in shades of green, gray green and creamy yellow. Variegation lessens and leaves may grow deformed in insufficient sunlight.

FICUS lyrata
"Fiddle Leaf Fig"
Moraceae
Medium to high indirect sunlight. Allow the soil to dry slightly between waterings. Medium humidity. Fertilize monthly. Propagate by air layering. Huge, handsome and dramatic foliage is characteristic to this fast grower. Clean foliage often with a damp cloth. Pinch off terminal growth when very young and occasionally thereafter if branching growth is desired. If new growth is small or deformed, the plant is probably not receiving sufficient sunlight. Native to Africa.

FICUS nekbudu (F. utilis)
"Zulu Fig Tree"
Moraceae
Medium sunlight. Allow the soil to become slightly dry between waterings. Medium humidity. Fertilize monthly. Propagate best by air layering. A somewhat uncommon variety with oval shaped leaves to 1 foot long. Dark green with vivid yellow primary veins and midrib. Usually slow growing when potted and indoors. Capable of growing into a large sized tree.

FICUS pumila (F. repens)
"Creeping Fig"
Moraceae
Medium to high sunlight. Keep the soil moist. Medium humidity. Fertilize monthly. Propagate by soft wood cuttings. A creeping variety with heart shaped leaves to 1 inch long. Its clinging and branching growth habits are similar to that of *Ivy*. Often used in shady outdoor locations for covering walls and buildings. Enjoys warm temperatures between 60 and 70 degrees. Grows well in terrariums where it will eventually climb the glass.

FICUS rubiginosa variegata
"Miniature Rubber Plant"
Moraceae
Medium sunlight. Keep the soil moist. Medium, high humidity. Fertilize half doses monthly. Propagate by air layering. Dark green oval shaped leaves to 3 inches long are irregularly splashed and painted with cream coloring. Somewhat slow growing and particular to environments. Enjoys warm temperatures but keep out of hot direct sunlight. Native to Australia.

FICUS sarmentosa
"Miniature Ivy"
Moraceae
Medium sunlight. Keep the soil moist. High humidity is best. Prefers warm temperatures to 75 degrees. Fertilize monthly. Propagate by rooting soft wood cuttings under glass for humidity. A fast growing miniature vine suitable for dish gardens or terrarium culture. Its rooting branches can also adhere themselves to glass and other objects, quickly forming a dense cover. The tiny leaves grow no larger than ½ inch in length. Native to Japan.

FITTONIA verschaffeltii
"Mosaic Plant"
Acanthaceae
Medium sunlight. Keep the soil moist. Prefers temperatures about 65 degrees. High humidity. Fertilize monthly. Propagate by softwood cuttings. Lovely red veining on a dull green, papery thin background makes a striking contrast. Popular as a terrarium plant as it does not enjoy dry or drafty locations. They also do fairly well in dish gardens where they receive additional humidity from the other plants. Native to Peru.

FITTONIA verschaffeltii argyroneura
"Nerve Plant"
Acanthaceae
Medium sunlight. Keep the soil moist. Prefers warm temperatures about 65 degrees. High humidity. Fertilize monthly. Propagate by soft wood cuttings. A creeping plant with an exotic display of fresh green foliage heavily laced with white veins. The oval leaves grow to four inches long. The hairy stems root at nodes if allowed to creep on moist soil. Use distilled water if leaves develop brown spots. Native to Peru.

GESNERIA cuneifolia
"Firecracker"
Gesneriaceae
Medium sunlight. Keep the soil moist. Medium humidity. Fertilize monthly with half doses. Propagate by seed or by soft wood cuttings. A charming, miniature that is grown for both foliage and flowers. Lovely little 1 inch tubular flowers are colored with bright yellow and red. The glossy, leathery leaves grow to 4 inches long. Blooms almost continuously. Removing spent blooms will encourage more. Branches when mature. Perfect for terrariums.

GIBASIS geniculata
"Tahitian Bridal Veil"
Commelinaceae
High sunlight. Keep the soil slightly moist and occasionally allow to become rather dry. Medium humidity. Fertilize monthly. Propagate easily by soft wood cuttings. Because of its downward or creeping growth habit, this popular plant is most often grown in hanging containers. The combination of the dense, fine foliage and the abundant, minute white flowers indeed appear to be a *"Bridal Veil"*. Related to *"Wandering Jew"*. Native to Tropical America.

GLECOMA hederaceae *"Ground Ivy"* Labiatae (below, left)
GLECOMA hederaceae variegata *"Variegated Ground Ivy"* (below, right)
Medium sunlight. Keep the soil moist. Medium humidity. Fertilize monthly. Propagate by seed, soft wood cuttings, soil layering or division. Creeping stems are distantly furnished with opposite, scalloped, to 1½ inch wide, kidney shaped leaves. Enjoys fresh air circulation.

GYNURA aurantiaca *"Velvet Plant"* Compositae (below, left)
GYNURA 'Sarmentosa' *"Purple Passion Plant"* (below, right)
Medium, high sunlight. Keep the soil moist. Medium humidity. Fertilize monthly. Propagate by soft wood cuttings or by soil layering. Upright growth eventually becomes pendulous with weight of foliage. The soft, to 4 inch long, leaves are completely covered with fine purple hairs. Excellent subjects for water culture or for artificial sunlight.

HAWORTHIA fasciata
"Zebra Haworthia"
Liliaceae
Medium sunlight. Allow the soil to become slightly dry between waterings. Medium humidity. Fertilize with half doses and discontinue completely September thru February. Propagate by offsets or runners. A very thin but lovely succulent plant. The spike-like leaves grow in a rosette to 3 inches in diameter. They are colored dark green and have rows of white warts on the undersides. Best suited for succulent dish gardens. Native to Africa.

HEDERA *"The Ivies" Araliaceae*

Probably the most widely grown vine in the homes of America today. *Hedera helix* and its cultivars, shown on these pages, represent only a few of the many that are actually available. They are capable of climbing walls and trees by rooted "feet" that grow from their stems. For indoor culture, they are grown in both hanging or standing containers. They are eager to be trained or shaped to suit your requirements. Pinch back, if desired, to encourage bushiness. They make good subjects for water culture. For optimum growth, provide medium to high sunlight. Keep the soil moist to slightly moist at all times. Medium humidity is enjoyed by all varieties. Fertilize monthly and decrease to half doses during colder months. Propagate easily by soft wood cuttings.

Hedera helix *"English Ivy'*

Hedera helix 'Calif. Needlepoint'

Hedera helix 'Curlilocks'

Hedera helix 'Fleur'

Hedera helix 'Glacier'

Hedera helix 'Hahns' selfbranching'

Hedera helix 'Scutifolia'

Hedera helix 'Shamrock'

HEIMERLIODENDRON brunonianum
'Variegatum'
"Pisonia"
Nyctaginaceae
Medium sunlight. Keep the soil moist. Medium humidity. Fertilize monthly. Propagate by air layering. A small tree like plant that grows to 6 feet. Leaves, to 8 inches, are attractively variegated in two shades of green with ivory splashed mostly in the margins. New growth has pinkish areas that later fade into ivory. A sport of *H. brunonianum* the *"Para Para"* tree. Native to New Zealand.

HEMIGRAPHIS colorata
"Red Ivy"
Acanthaceae
Medium to low sunlight. Keep the soil only slightly moist. Prefers warm temperatures. High humidity. Fertilize monthly. Propagate by healthy soft wood cuttings. The long, 2" to 4" heart shaped leaves are faintly cast with metallic purple. Requires occasional "topping" or pinching back to keep foliage well shaped. You can also pot two or three plants together for a fuller foliage effect. Native of Java.

HEMIGRAPHIS "Exotica"
"Waffle Plant"
Acanthaceae
Medium to low sunlight. Keep the soil only slightly moist. Prefers warm temperatures to 80 degrees. High humidity is best. Fertilize monthly. Propagate by softwood cuttings. Attractive, dark green, very puckered and unusual leaves make this a popular plant for the home. Foliage has a slight metallic cast but not as prominent as *"Red Ivy"*. It will usually tolerate a medium humidity. Native to New Guinea.

HOYA carnosa variegata
"Variegated Wax Plant"
Asclepiadaceae
Medium sunlight. Allow the soil to become slightly dry between waterings. Medium humidity. Fertilize monthly and discontinue completely September thru January. Propagate best by soil layering. A stiff, vining plant with thick, waxy leaves to 3 inches long. Colored deep green with cream to pinkish red edges. Clusters of white, star shaped flowers. Good for water culture.

HYPOCYRTA glabra
"Goldfish Plant"
Gesneriaceae
Medium sunlight. Keep the soil moist. Medium, high humidity. Fertilize monthly and decrease to half doses during colder months. Propagate by seed or by soft wood cuttings. A lovely little trailing vine that is prized for both foliage and flowers. Opposite, dark green leaves are thick, extremely shiny and grow to about 1¼ inches long. Summer blooming flowers are tubular with an inflated, pouch like, lower lip. Cut back tips after blooming ceases.

HYPOESTES sanguinolenta
"Freckle Face" or "Pink Polka Dot"
Acanthaceae
Medium sunlight. Keep the soil moist. High humidity. Prefers warm temperatures. Fertilize monthly. Propagate by fresh stem cuttings. This pretty little plant is an absolute must for the colorful terrarium. It is capable of growing 18" high but occasional trimming of the terminal growth will keep it compact and full. In proper sunlight, it will produce tiny purple flowers. Insufficient watering can cause the plant to wilt and lose its lower leaves.

IMPATIENS
"Touch-me-not"
Balsaminaceae
Medium to high sunlight. Keep the soil moist. Medium, high humidity. Fertilize monthly when showing new growth or blooming. Propagate by seed or soft wood cuttings. Easy to grow, blooming plants that are suitable for indoor culture if fresh air circulation is present. Some types have variegated foliage and most have simple flowers in a wide range of colors. Most nurseries carry a selection of different varieties. Often reseeds itself.

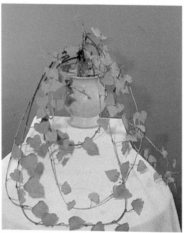

IPOMOEA batatas
"Sweet Potato Vine"
Convolvulaceae
This is a fun project for gardeners of all ages as it is inexpensive and relatively quick to mature. Use toothpicks to hold a common Sweet Potato $2/3$ out of a container of water. It makes no difference whether you place the side or the end in the water. Keep the water covering $1/3$ of the potato. Root growth should appear in a few days and foliage should grow in a month or less. It will continue to produce foliage for months before dying back.

IRESINE herbstii
"Beefsteak Plant"
Amaranthaceae
High sunlight. Keep the soil moist. Medium humidity. Fertilize monthly. Propagate by soft wood cuttings. Commonly used in many areas outdoors as an annual bedding plant. Almost round, spoon like leaves are slightly indented at the tips. Stems, primarily veins and midribs are colored deep pink on a dark purple background. Pinch back occasionally to keep full and bushy. Native to Brazil.

IRESINE herbstii 'Aureo-reticulata'
"Chicken Gizzard"
Amaranthaceae
High sunlight. Keep the soil moist. Medium humidity. Fertilize monthly. Propagate by soft wood cuttings. Very similar in growth habits to the *"Beefsteak Plant."* Stems are red. Primary veins and midrib are bright yellow on a fresh green background. Leaves are notched at tips. *Iresine* may be used in terrariums for color. They will tolerate lower sunlight conditions, however, slow and spindly growth may result. Pinch for bushiness.

KALANCHOE blossfeldiana
"Christmas Kalanchoe"　　'Tom Thumb'
Crassulaceae
High sunlight. Allow the soil to become slightly dry between waterings. Medium humidity. Fertilize half doses every 3 months. Propagate by leaf or soft wood cuttings. A compact, dwarfed succulent. Usually available, in bloom, during the holidays. Leaves, to 2 inches long, are very glossy, and almost flat. Beautiful clusters of simple, red flowers bloom on stalks above foliage. Place outdoors in a warm, almost full sun location June thru August to encourage budset.

KALANCHOE manginii
Crassulaceae
High sunlight. Allow the soil to become slightly dry between waterings. Medium humidity. Fertilize half doses every 3 months. Propagate by leaf or soft wood cuttings. A somewhat pendulous variety that is often displayed in hanging containers. Spoon shaped leaves are smooth and waxy. Pretty, cream colored flowers are tinged carmine and hang like bells. Pot all *Kalanchoe* in a fast draining soil mixture. This can be blended of $2/3$ regular potting soil and $1/3$ coarse builders sand. Native to Madagascar.

KALANCHOE pumila
"Dwarf Purple Kalanchoe"
Crassulaceae
High sunlight. Allow the soil to become slightly dry between waterings. Medium humidity. Fertilize half doses every 3 months. Propagate by leaf or soft wood cuttings. A succulent with powdered, gray green leaves. Edges are tinged with purple and scalloped at the tips. Growth is bushy to about 6 inches high. Clusters of flowers are deep pink. Shear tops back when blooming ceases. Native to Madagascar.

LAMIUM galeobdolon variegatum
"Silver Nettle Vine" or *"Archangel"*
Labiatae
Medium sunlight. Allow the soil to become slightly dry between waterings. Medium humidity. Fertilize monthly. Propagate by soft wood cuttings or by soil layering. A beautifully colored and fast growing, creeping vine. Commonly displayed in hanging containers. Opposite, heart shaped leaves, to 2 inches long, are fresh green and variegated with greenish silver. Prefers cooler temperatures between 45 and 65 degrees.

LIRIOPE muscari 'Variegata'
"Variegated Lily Turf"
Liliaceae
Medium sunlight. Keep the soil moist. Medium humidity. Fertilize monthly. Propagate by division. A colorful grass like plant that spreads by underground branches. The thin blade shaped leaves, to 18 inches long, are fresh green with stripes of cream, especially in the margins. Related and similar to *Ophiopogon and Chlorophytum*. Spikes of pretty violet flowers bloom high above foliage. Native to China and Japan.

LYSIMACHIA nummularia
"Moneywort" or "Creeping Jennie"
Primulaceae
Medium sunlight. Keep the soil moist. Medium humidity. Fertilize monthly. Propagate by soft wood cuttings or by soil layering. A creeping or hanging plant with stems to 2 feet long. Leaves are almost completely round, opposite, fresh green and distantly spaced. Grows best with fresh air circulation. Small, yellow flowers bloom during warm months if grown in adequate sunlight.

MARANTA leuconeura erythroneura
"Red Veined Prayer Plant"
Marantaceae
Medium sunlight. Allow the soil to become slightly dry between waterings. Medium humidity. Prefers warm areas to 80 degrees. Fertilize monthly and decrease in winter. Propagate by division. All *Marantas* fold their leaves upward at night. It is said that the reason for this is to "funnel" dew from the leaves down on to the roots. Other varieties are commonly available and equally as unusual. Native to Brazil.

MIKANIA ternata
"Plush Vine"
Compositae
Medium sunlight. Keep the soil moist. Medium humidity. Fertilize monthly. Propagate by soft wood cuttings. Most striking foliage plant consisting of dark green velvety and slightly hairy leaves and stems. Good plant for contrasting with others or for adding uniqueness to your collection. Related to *Gynura,* the *"Velvet Plants"* which also have similar characteristics. Native to Brazil.

MIMOSA pudica
"Sensitivity Plant" or "Touch me not"
Leguminosae
High sunlight. Keep the soil slightly moist. Medium humidity. Fertilize monthly after sprouts have formed true leaves. Propagate by seed. This plant is usually grown as a novelty. It is actually a weed and not especially favored for its foliage but for its fascinating ability to rapidly droop its leaves when touched. This is an annual that is capable of growing to 18" high. Originally from Brazil.

NANDINA domestica
"Heavenly bamboo"
Berberidaceae
Medium to high sunlight. Keep the soil moist. Medium to high humidity. Fertilize monthly if pot grown. Propagate from seed or soft wood cuttings. Trileaflets held on thin delicate stems falsely imitate a true *Bamboo*. Most commonly used in terrariums when young. Leaves have red-brown tinge when new and when grown in adequate sunlight. Native to South East Asia.

NICODEMIA diversifolia
"Indoor Oak"
Loganiaceae
Medium, high sunlight. Keep the soil moist. Medium humidity. Fertilize monthly and decrease to half doses during colder months. Propagate by soft wood cuttings March thru August. A small shrub that can grow to a height of 2 feet. Leaves, to 2 inches long, are similar in appearance to those of the true *Oak* tree. They are fresh green in color and have a lustrous sheen. Pinching back terminal growth will keep full and bushy. Native to Madagascar.

OPHIOPOGON japonicus
"Mondo Grass" or "Snake's Beard"
Liliaceae

Medium to high sunlight. Keep the soil moist. Medium humidity. Fertilize monthly. Propagate by division. Long, thin, dark green leaves grow to a foot long and usually measure no more than ¼" wide when grown in the home. Growing underground stolens which send up new foliage eventually become full mounds of leaf blades. The variegated variety, which is becoming commonly available, has very attractive white stripes. Native to the Orient.

ORCHIDS
Orchidaceae

Medium to high filtered sunlight. Allow the growing medium to become slightly dry between waterings. Medium, high humidity. Use Fish fertilizer monthly during periods of growth and flowering. Propagate by seed or division depending upon the variety. Generally prefer cooler temperatures, especially during the night. Types of growth, foliage and flowers vary widely. Some are very large and some are small enough to grow in terrariums. Many are epiphitic. Pot in shredded firbark or Osmunda root.

Paphiopedilum—Lady Slipper

Orchid - Cattleya

Orchid - Cymbidium

ORNITHOGALUM caudatum
"Pregnant Onion" or "False Sea Onion"
Liliaceae
High sunlight. Keep the soil slightly moist and allow to become almost dry between waterings. Medium humidity. Fertilize monthly. Propagate by removing and rooting the bulbs that grow on the bulb of the "mother plant". This is a most unusual foliage plant that is grown for its long, drooping, strap-like leaves and a large, to five inch diameter bulb at the base. The bulb, which can produce many bulbs per year, is planted mostly above soil. Native to Africa.

OXALIS hedysaroides rubra (upper)
O. martiana 'Aureo-reticulata' (lower)
Oxalidaceae
Medium to high sunlight. Keep the soil moist. Medium humidity. Fertilize when productive and showing new growth. Often called *"Shamrocks"* or *"Clover"* and having compound leaves that are divided into 3 or more leaflets. They are grown for both flowers and often colorful leaflets that close at dusk. Many grow from rhizomes or tubers and must have a dormant period, after blooming, of less water and sunlight and cooler temperatures.

PANDANUS veitchii
"Variegated Screw Pine"
Pandanaceae
Medium sunlight. Allow the soil to become slightly dry between waterings. Medium humidity. Fertilize monthly with half doses. Propagate by removing the offsets that sprout from the base. Similar in appearance to the *Dracaenas*. Long, narrow, stiff leaves grow to 2 feet in length and have toothed edges. They are arranged in a spiral at the top of a naked stem. Drops aerial roots when mature. Native to Polynesia.

PALMS and CYCAS revoluta (A Palm like plant)

Palms are tropical and dramatic decorator trees. They are very enduring and tolerant of indoor conditions. Some have a single trunk and can be potted individually or 2 to 3 of varying sizes may be planted together for fullness. Others vigorously produce suckers (offsets) that keep the lower portion full with foliage. Palms are delicate plants in that they are not accustomed to extremely hot sunlight. They can be easily sunburned if placed too near a window with direct exposure. They grow well in crowded containers. Repotting is usually necessary about every 2 to 3 years. They prefer a fast draining but moisture retaining soil mixture. It is important that they not be allowed to either stand in water or to become excessively dry. Provide a dormant period during colder months by lessening the frequency of watering and by reducing the strength of fertilizer.

CARYOTA 'plumosa'
"Fishtail Palm"
Palmae
Medium sunlight. Keep the soil moist. Medium humidity. Fertilize monthly and decrease to ¼ doses September thru February. Propagate by seed or suckers (offsets). A unique *Palm* tree with branched stems. Leaflets have irregular, jagged edges as though they were torn. Produces vigorous suckers from its base. A lovely decorator plant that is especially useful for tropical effects. Capable of exceeding 20 feet when mature. Native to Ceylon.

CHAMAEDOREA elegans 'bella'
"Neanthe Bella Palm"
Palmae
Low to medium sunlight. Keep the soil moist. Medium humidity. Fertilize monthly and decrease to ¼ doses September thru February. Propagate by seed. A variety small enough to spend its first two years in a terrarium or dish garden. Extremely tolerant of all adverse conditions except hot, direct sunlight. Grows to about 2½ feet tall. *C. elegans* is a variety, almost identical in appearance, and is capable of exceeding 7 feet in height. Native to Tropical America.

CHAMAEDORIA seifrizii
"Reed Palm"
Palmae
Medium sunlight. Keep the soil moist. Medium humidity. Fertilize monthly and decrease to ¼ doses September thru February. Propagate by seed or suckers (offsets). A choice variety that becomes large, but not overwhelming as an indoor plant. Develops a naked reed like stem with a crown of foliage at the top. If cared for properly, almost continuous, suckering growth will keep the lower portion full with foliage. Keep out of hot, direct sunlight. Native to Mexico.

CYCAS revoluta
"Sago Palm"
Cycadaceae
Medium to high indirect sunlight. Allow the soil to become slightly dry between waterings. Medium humidity. Fertilize with half doses and discontinue completely September thru February. Propagate by seed or suckers (offsets) when dormant. The ferny foliage of this prehistoric plant is symmetrically arranged and much resembles a *Palm*. Produces a complete new set of leaves, all at once, every 1 or 2 years. Slow growing. Native from Japan to Java.

HOWEIA forsteriana
"Kentia Palm" or *"Paradise Palm"*
Palmae
Medium sunlight. Keep the soil moist. Medium humidity. Fertilize monthly and decrease to ¼ doses September thru February. Propagate by seed. Large, stately and well accepted decorator plant. Capable of growing to 60 feet high in natural habitat. Drops off lower leaves as it grows, leaving a slender trunk. Pot in fast draining soil and never allow to become absolutely dry. Seeds were first imported from Lord Howe Island about one hundred years ago.

RHAPIS excelsa
"Lady Palm"
Palmae
Medium sunlight. Keep the soil moist. Medium humidity. Fertilize monthly and decrease to ¼ doses September thru February. Propagate by seed or suckers (offsets). Crowns of fan like leaves eventually grow to 1 foot long. The slender stems are clothed with heavy fibre. Continuous suckers keep lower portion full with foliage. *R. humilis* is very similar except the tips of the leaflets are not "clipped." Native to Japan.

RHAPIS excelsa 'Variegata'
"Variegated Lady Palm;;
Palmae
Medium sunlight. Keep the soil moist. Medium, high humidity. Fertilize monthly and decrease to ¼ doses September thru February. Propagate by seed or suckers (offsets). Unusual and rather rare to the United States. Somewhat slower growing than *R. excelsa*. Very generously striped with a yellowish, cream coloring. Stems are covered with fibers and leaflet tips are "clipped." A true specimen plant, valuable to collectors of the unique. Native to Japan.

PELLIONIA pulchra
"Satin Pellionia"
Urticaceae
Medium sunlight. Keep the soil moist. Medium, high humidity. Fertilize monthly and decrease to half doses October thru January. Propagate by soft wood cuttings. A dense, creeping foliage plant with long purplish stems. Leaves are oval and grow to almost 1½ inches in length. They are colored medium green with dark purple veining. Undersides are gray green with purple veining. Best suited for glass house culture. Native to Vietnam.

PEPEROMIA Piperaceae

Most all members of this group are excellent plants for the amateur indoor gardener. They are easy to grow and are tolerant of indoor growing conditions. The stems are usually somewhat succulent or crisp with water. The leaves of some varieties are clear with the pigment or coloring on the underside allowing you to see right through to the back of the leaf. The many different varieties offer all types of growth; hanging, creeping, upright and branching or rosette. All types of *Peperomia* are easily propagated. Soft wood cuttings can be "rooted" in water.

PEPEROMIA caperata
"Emerald Ripple"
Piperaceae
Medium sunlight. Keep the soil slightly moist. Medium humidity. Fertilize monthly. Propagate by leaf cuttings or by leaf-stem cuttings. A very attractive and popular rosette of dark green, heart shaped corrugated leaves borne on slender reddish stems. Minute flowers grow on "spikes" high above foliage. Turn pot occasionally for full growth on all sides of the plant. Grows well in terrariums. Native to Brazil.

PEPEROMIA griseo-argentea
"Ivy Peperomia"
Piperaceae
Medium sunlight. Keep the soil slightly moist. Medium humidity. Fertilize monthly. Propagate by leaf cuttings or by leaf-stem cuttings. Low growing rosette similar to *P. Caperata* yet somewhat less corrugated. The rounded, heart shaped leaves are colored shiny silver. Stems red and greenish white flower spikes are characteristic. Native to Brazil.

PEPEROMIA griseo-argentea 'Blackie'
Piperaceae
Medium sunlight. Keep the soil slightly moist. Medium humidity. Fertilize monthly. Propagate by leaf cuttings or by leaf-stem cuttings. Dense rosette of slightly cupped and deeply veined, rounded, heart shaped leaves borne on slender stems. Leaf margins are also finely rippled. Medium green foliage color darkens with age.

PEPEROMIA obtusifolia
"Baby Rubber Plant" or "Pepperface"
Piperaceae
Medium sunlight. Keep the soil slightly moist. Medium humidity. Fertilize monthly. Propagate by leaf, leaf-stem or soft wood cuttings. Large, succulent leaves on up to one foot long stems make this plant among the most popular of all *Peperomias*. Leaves are clear with pigment on the underside. Branching of the stems can be initiated by cutting off the terminal growth. Native to Venezuela.

PEPEROMIA 'Variegata'
"Variegated Peperomia"
Piperaceae
Medium sunlight. Keep the soil slightly moist. Medium humidity. Fertilize monthly. Propagate by leaf, leaf-stem, or softwood cuttings. A richly variegated variety and extremely hardy plant with very shiny leaves to three inches long, splashed with cream and yellow coloring, predominatly near margins. Long stems, being rather succulent, can be easily broken. Leaf is clear with coloring on the underside. Stems reddish-brown.

PEPEROMIA orba
"Princess Astrid Peperomia"
Piperaceae
Medium sunlight. Keep the soil slightly moist. Medium humidity. Fertilize monthly. Propagate by leaf, leaf-stem or softwood cuttings. Dense, bushy growth on branching stems is characteristic. Leaves are fresh green and waxy to two inches long on mature plant. Branches can be pinched back to keep growth compact or they can be allowed to trail. Originally from Sweden.

PEPEROMIA polybotrya
"Coin Leaf Peperomia"
Piperaceae
Medium sunlight. Keep the soil slightly moist. Medium humidity. Fertilize monthly. Propagate by leaf, leaf-stem or by soft wood cuttings. Unusual and somewhat uncommon variety with erect stem. Rounded leaves with a pointed tip are supported by slender green stems. Can be staked, if desired, to prevent the crisp stem from being accidentally broken. Native to Columbia.

PEPEROMIA prostrata
Piperaceae
Medium sunlight. Keep the soil moist. Fertilize monthly. Propagate by leaf cuttings, softwood cuttings or by soil layering. This variety can be planted in a small pot and allowed to cascade over the sides or it can be used effectively as a ground cover in terrariums. It is a very fast grower for its size; however, the attractively colored leaves are no larger than ¼" in diameter. A must for those interested in miniature plants. Native to Columbia.

PEPEROMIA rubella
"Yerba Linda"
Piperaceae
Medium sunlight. Keep the soil slightly moist. Medium humidity. Fertilize monthly. Propagate by leaf or softwood cuttings. Attractive, bushy little plant with densely branched, reddish and hairy stems. Layers of tiny, oval leaves, reddish beneath, faintly marked with silvery lines are characteristic. Pinch back occasionally, if desired, to keep growth full. Primarily native to Mexico.

PEPEROMIA sandersii
"Watermelon Peperomia"
Piperaceae
Medium sunlight. Keep the soil slightly moist. Medium humidity. Fertilize monthly. Propagate by leaf or leaf-stem cuttings. Low growing rosette form with very unusual silver leaf markings radiating from leaf center to point. Leaves are glossy and usually grow no larger than three inches. Stems are reddish and slender. Minute flowers on long spikes above foliage. Grows to nine inches high. Popular as a terrarium plant. Native to Brazil.

PEPEROMIA scandens
"Philodendron Peperomia"
Piperaceae
Medium sunlight. Keep the soil slightly moist. Medium humidity. Fertilize monthly. Propagate by leaf, leaf-stem or softwood cuttings. Light green, creased and pointed leaves widely spaced on green or reddish stems. Commonly used as a hanging plant because of spreading or creeping growth habit. Pinch back occasionally to keep full as it has a tendency to grow spindly. Native of Peru.

PEPEROMIA scandens 'Variegata'
"Variegated Philodendron Leaf"
Piperaceae

Medium sunlight. Keep the soil slightly moist. Medium humidity. Fertilize monthly. Propagate by leaf, leaf-stem or soft wood cuttings. Similar to *P. scandens* in growth except leaves are colored creamy green with irregular, cream colored margins. An excellent plant for easy care in a hanging container.

PHILODENDRONS Araceae

Probably the most accepted and widely available of all decorator plants. They are grown for the beauty of their large, leathery and often very glossy leaves. They are divided, by growth habits, into two main groups; trailing and self-heading. All are climbers. *Philodendrons,* as well as *Aglaonema, Dieffenbachia, Scindapsus, Syngonium* and several others are Aroids. Their blooms usually consist of a spadix and spathe. The spadix is a spike like growth which is covered with minute, petalless flowers. The spathe is a leaf like organ that surrounds or opens below the spadix. *Calla lilies, Spathiphyllum* and *Anthuriums* are familiar examples of these unusual blooms. The climbing types of *Philodendrons* produce aerial roots at the joints or nodes. These cord like roots are moisture seeking and are capable of growing very long. They absorb moisture from both the air and the soil, if touching. In general, they prefer warm temperatures between 60 and 75 degrees. Pot in your regular soil mixture. Most will also tolerate lower sunlight conditions.

PHILODENDRON andreanum
"Velour Philodendron"
Araceae

Low to medium, indirect or filtered sunlight. Keep the soil moist. High humidity. Fertilize monthly with half doses. Propagate by soft wood cuttings or by air layering. A beautiful climbing variety that is unfortunately best suited for glass house culture. Elongated, heart shaped leaves grow to about 12 inches long. They are very luxurious and velvety in texture. Colored dark olive with greenish, white veining. Native to South America.

118

PHILODENDRON x 'Burgundy'
Araceae

Medium sunlight. Keep the soil moist. Medium humidity. Fertilize monthly with half doses. Propagate by soft wood cuttings or by soil layering. A recently developed hybrid that demonstrates excellent qualities as an indoor plant. Leaves grow to 12 inches in length and are dark green in color. New growth, veins on undersides and portions of the stems are colored deep burgundy. Semi-climbing growth habits. Requires staking.

PHILODENDRON domesticum
"Elephants Ear"
Araceae

Medium sunlight. Keep the soil moist. Medium humidity. Fertilize monthly with half doses. Propagate by soft wood cuttings or by air layering. Also commonly referred to as *P. hastatum*. A variety, well established as a house plant. Fast growing with climbing habits. Elongated, heart shaped leaves are medium green in color and grow to 12 inches long. Requires staking. Abundant, indirect or filtered sunlight will keep the foliage full. Native to Brazil.

PHILODENDRON x 'Florida'
Araceae

Medium sunlight. Keep the soil moist. Medium humidity. Fertilize monthly with half doses. Propagate by soft wood cuttings or by air layering. An easy to grow hybrid with leaves that are divided into 5 main sections. They are colored deep green with lighter green midribs. Stems are very slender and should be supported on a moss stick. Rotate the pot occasionally as it, along with most other *Philodendrons*, will quickly seek its source of sunlight. Do not allow to become excessively dry.

PHILODENDRON oxycardium
"Heartleaf Philodendron"
Araceae

Medium sunlight. Keep the soil moist. Medium humidity. Fertilize monthly with half doses. Propagate easily from soft wood cuttings. The most common of all *Philodendrons*. A fast growing, climbing variety. Stems are capable of exceeding 20 feet in length. Leaves are dark green, heart shaped and grow to 6 inches long. Tolerates insufficient sunlight and warm rooms. Good subject for water culture. Native to Jamaica, Puerto Rico and Central America.

PHILODENDRON panduraeforme
"Fiddleleaf Philodendron"
Araceae

Medium sunlight. Keep the soil moist. Medium humidity. Fertilize monthly with half doses. Propagate by soft wood cuttings or by air layering. Unique, deep green and leathery, "fiddle" shaped leaves. A popular variety because of its dense foliage and its tolerance of very low sunlight conditions. Stake or grow in a mossed basket for best results. Somewhat slow growing. Native to Brazil.

PHILODENDRON pertusum
"Splitleaf Philodendron"
Araceae

Medium sunlight. Keep the soil moist. Medium humidity. Fertilize monthly with half doses and discontinue completely October thru January. Propagate by soft wood cuttings or by air layering. Botanically, this plant is actually an immature form of the huge *Monstera deliciosia*. The late appearance of additional perforations in the leaves has caused it to be referred to by two names. Develops a large trunk and long, moisture seeking aerial roots.

PILEA cadierei
"Aluminum Plant"
Urticaceae
Medium sunlight. Keep the soil moist to slightly moist at all times. Medium humidity. Enjoys warm rooms. Fertilize monthly. Propagate by soft wood cuttings. Unique metallic, aluminum color uniformly patterned over light green background is characteristic. Growing in a small bush form with up to three inch leaves. Will drop lower leaves if allowed to become very dry. Originally from Vietnam.

PILEA depressa
"Miniature Peperomia"
Urticaceae
Medium sunlight. Allow the soil to become slightly dry between waterings. Medium humidity. Fertilize monthly with half doses and discontinue completely October thru January. Propagate by soft wood cuttings or by soil layering. A creeping succulent that is usually displayed in a hanging container. May also be used as a ground cover in terrariums. The tiny, ¼ inch, almost round leaves are thick and waxy. Native to Puerto Rico.

PILEA involucrata
"Panamiga" or *"Friendship Plant"*
Urticaceae
Medium sunlight. Keep the soil moist. Medium humidity. Fertilize monthly with half doses and discontinue completely October thru January. Propagate best by soft wood cuttings. A popular hanging or trailing vine of easy culture. The fresh green and very quilted leaves, to 1¾ inches long, become reddish brown when grown in strong sunlight. Pinch back occasionally to keep dense. Reddish flowers bloom in leaf joints. Native to Peru.

PILEA microphylla (muscosa)
"Artillery Plant"
Urticaceae

Medium sunlight. Allow the soil to become slightly dry between waterings. Medium to high humidity. Fertilize monthly. Propagate by soft wood cuttings. Its name is derived from the pollen explosions that are given off by the flowers when dry and disturbed. They are good fern-like plants for terrariums. Capable of growing to 18 inches in height when mature. Two other varieties, of similar appearance and culture, are shown below.

Pilea microphylla compacta

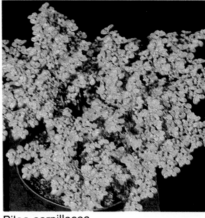

Pilea serpillacea

PILEA 'Moon Valley'
"Moon Valley"
Urticaceae

Medium indirect sunlight. Allow the soil to become slightly dry between waterings. Medium to high humidity. Fertilize monthly. Propagate by soft wood cuttings. Extremely quilted foliage makes this plant an instant eye-catcher. Because of its culture and contrasting green and brown coloring, it is perfect as a terrarium plant. Occasionally pinch off terminal growth for branching as they tend to grow leggy.

PILEA nummulariifolia
"Creeping Charlie"
Urticaceae
Medium sunlight. Keep the soil moist. Medium humidity. Fertilize monthly with half doses and discontinue completely October thru January. Propagate by soft wood cuttings or by soil layering. A miniature, creeping ground cover. Thin reddish stems root into the soil as they spread. Light green leaves are deeply quilted, slightly hairy and round. Can be potted singly or used in terrariums and dish gardens.

PILEA repens
"Black Leaf Panamiga"
Urticaceae
Medium sunlight. Keep the soil moist. Medium, high humidity. Fertilize monthly with half doses and discontinue completely October thru January. Propagate by soft wood cuttings. Dark green to brownish leaves are almost round and grow to 1½ inches. The surface is quilted and shiny with scalloped edges. Undersides are slightly hairy and purplish. Growth is spreading to 8 inches in height. Native to Mexico.

PILEA 'Silver Tree'
"Silver and Bronze"
Urticaceae
Medium sunlight. Keep the soil moist. Medium humidity. Fertilize monthly with half doses and discontinue completely October thru January. Propagate by soft wood cuttings. A relatively new variety with very glossy foliage. Has bushy growth to 1 foot tall. Leaves are dark green and have a broad center band of silver. Occasionally pinch back terminal growth to keep foliage full and compact. Native to the Caribbean.

PIPER crocatum
"Peruvian Ornamental Pepper"
Piperaceae
Medium sunlight. Keep the soil moist. Medium, high humidity. Fertilize monthly. Propagate by soft wood cuttings. Glossy green leathery leaves to 4 inches long are painted along the veins with a soft pearl pink color. Undersides of the leaves and stems are purple and covered with tiny clear beads of exudation. Do not allow to become completely dry as leaves may drop off. Native to Peru.

PLECTRANTHUS australis
"Swedish Ivy" or "Creeping Charlie"
Labiatae
Medium sunlight. Keep the soil moist. Medium humidity. Fertilize monthly. Propagate by soft wood cuttings. A vigorously growing, creeping or hanging vine with lush, almost round and succulent leaves. Terminal growth must be pinched back to keep full. Remove superfluous blooms as they form. Extremely popular along the West Coast where often grown in shaded area outdoors. Originally from the South Pacific Area.

PLECTRANTHUS myrianthus
"Variegated Creeping Charlie"
Labiatae
Medium sunlight. Keep the soil moist. Medium humidity. Fertilize monthly. Propagate by soft wood cuttings. Similar to *Plectranthus australis* with the exception of variegated, cream on green leaves. They have the same culture and are very contrasting when potted together. Terminal growth of this variety or mutation must also be pinched back to keep full.

PLECTRANTHUS ciliatus
Labiatae
Medium sunlight. Keep the soil moist. Medium humidity. Fertilize monthly. Propagate by soft wood cuttings under a humid enclosure. Most all *Plectranthus* enjoy warm rooms to 75 degrees. Because of similar appearance, it is often mistaken for *Pilea repens* which has more rounded leaves. Erect growth eventually becomes pendulous unless pinched back. Finely corrugated leaves are glossy green with purplish veins. Plant in a fast draining soil mix. Native to Southern Africa.

PLECTRANTHUS coleoides
'Marginatus'

"Candle Plant"
Labiatae
Medium to high sunlight. Keep the soil moist. Medium humidity. Fertilize monthly. Propagate by soft wood cuttings. A small, upright and freely branching shrub. The soft leaves are light green with white coloring in the margins. Pinch off the blooms as they form. Insufficient sunlight may cause leaves to drop or turn brown. It is ideally a patio plant as it enjoys good air circulation.

PLECTRANTHUS oertendahlii
"Prostrate Coleus"
Labiatae
Medium sunlight. Keep the soil moist. Medium humidity. Fertilize monthly. Propagate by soft wood cuttings under a humid enclosure. A lovely trailer, suitable for hanging containers. Fresh green, almost round, leaves are thick with moisture and have silvery veining. Leaf edges have a slight tinge of purple. The surface also has very minute hairs. If necessary, pinch out terminal growth to initiate branching.

PLECTRANTHUS tomentosus
"Succulent Coleus"
Labiatae
Medium sunlight. Allow the soil to become slightly dry between waterings. Medium humidity. Fertilize half doses monthly. Propagate by soft wood cuttings. Dull, light green leaves and stems are juicy and covered with a very fine fuzz. Growing into a dense little shrub if terminal growth is occasionally pinched off. Native to South Africa.

PODOCARPUS macrophyllus 'Maki'
"Southern Yew"
Podocarpaceae
High sunlight. Keep the soil moist. Medium humidity. Fertilize monthly. Propagate by seed or hardwood cuttings in Autumn. This is actually a tree capable of growing to 50 feet high. Since it is very slow growing, it can be potted and kept indoors for many years. Lends itself well to pruning and shaping. They do not enjoy transplanting and should be potted in fast draining soil.

POLYSCIAS balfouriana marginata
"Variegated Balfour Aralia"
Araliaceae
Medium sunlight. Keep the soil moist to slightly moist. Medium humidity. Fertilize monthly with half doses. Propagate by soft wood cuttings. An elegant, tree like shrub that grows indoors to about 4 feet tall. Branches freely and will stay dense if grown in adequate indirect or filtered sunlight. Leaves are usually divided into 3, almost round, irregularly scalloped leaflets. Fresh green coloring with white margins. Native to the French island of New Caledonia.

POLYSCIAS balfouriana 'Pennockii'
"White Aralia"
Araliaceae
Medium sunlight. Keep the soil moist to slightly moist. Medium, high humidity. Fertilize monthly with half doses. Propagate by soft wood cuttings. A beautiful cultivar with leaves exotically splotched and colored fresh green and cream. They are oval shaped, slightly corrugated and grow to about 4 inches long. Shrub like growth to 4 or 5 feet tall. A rather hearty plant that grows well in most homes but will not tolerate very dry air.

POLYSCIAS fruticosa 'Elegans'
"Ming Aralia" or *"Parsley Panax"*
Araliaceae
High indirect sunlight. Keep the soil moist to slightly moist. Medium humidity. Fertilize monthly with half doses. Propagate by soft wood cuttings. A small tree like shrub with very finely divided and cut leaflets. Developes a rather thick and somewhat gnarled trunk. Most commonly grown in pots, however, small specimens will thrive in a terrarium. Not an extremely fast grower. Suffers in low humidity. Native to Polynesia.

POLYSCIAS paniculata 'Variegata'
"Variegated Roseleaf Panax"
Araliaceae
High filtered or indirect sunlight. Keep the soil moist to slightly moist. Medium, high humidity. Fertilize monthly with half doses. Propagate by soft wood cuttings. An *"Aralia"* with dense, bushy growth habits. The deep green leaflets are variegated with cream and edged with soft teeth. They appear very much to be from a rose bush. Keep away from central heating drafts. Soil should be well drained.

PSEUDERANTHEMUM atropurpurem tricolor
Acanthaceae

Medium sunlight. Keep the soil moist to slightly moist. Medium, high humidity. Fertilize monthly with half doses and discontinue completely September thru January. Propagate by soft wood cuttings under a humid enclosure. Deep green leaves, to 4 inches long, are irregularly splashed with metallic purple, cream and beige. Shrubby growth habits. Related to the colorful, *Aphelandra, Fittonia, Hemigraphis* and *Sanchezia*. Native to Polynesia.

RHOEO spathacea
"Moses in the Boat"
Commelinaceae

High indirect sunlight. Keep the soil moist. Medium humidity. Fertilize half doses monthly. Propagate by seed or easiest by offsets. Its name is derived from small flowers in boat shaped bracts that bloom near the bases of the leaves. The dark green foliage has contrasting bright purple undersides. Rather tolerant of insufficient sunlight and the forgetful waterer.

RHOEO spathacea 'Vittata'
"Variegated Boat Lily"
Commelinaceae

Medium to high indirect sunlight. Allow the soil to become slightly dry between waterings. Medium humidity. Fertilize half doses monthly. Propagate by offsets. Fine yellow stripes decorate the surface of this striking variety. The undersides are bright purple. Small flowers near the stem. New leaves that grow small or with less variegation could indicate insufficient sunlight.

SAINTPAULIA hybrids *"African Violets"* Gesneriaceae

A very charming and desirable group of small house plants. They are of easy culture and seem to actually enjoy blooming. Thousands of hybrids have been developed since the species was originally discovered, in Africa, in 1892. They grow in rosette form with the exception of some trailers. Leaves overlap and are spoon shaped, ruffled, curled, scalloped, and convoluted in many ways. Clusters of bright or pastel colored flowers bloom almost year round. Most any color and type of flower combination imaginable, is available. The hybrids shown vary widely and are representative of their many different characteristics. *African Violets,* as most *Gesneriads,* are low energy bloomers. They attain their most perfect shape and bloom most vigorously when somewhat pot bound. They are best confined, for their entire life, to a 4 inch pot. Rotate the pots occasionally as the leaves may seek the source of sunlight. Provide a medium amount of filtered or indirect sunlight. Keep the soil moist but not wet. High humidity is preferred, however, medium is usually adequate. Fertilize monthly with half doses. Propagate easily by stem and leaf cuttings. Premixed soils, blended especially for *African Violets,* are readily available.

Saintpaulia 'Caretree'

Saintpaulia 'Coral Skies'

Saintpaulia 'High Stepper'

Saintpaulia 'Jayme'

Saintpaulia 'Blizzard Supreme'

Saintpaulia 'Blue Dolphin'

Saintpaulia 'Festival'

Saintpaulia 'Garnet Elf'

Saintpaulia 'Mark'

Saintpaulia 'Merry Blue'

Saintpaulia 'Orchid Melody'

Saintpaulia 'Pocono'

Saintpaulia 'Poodle Top'

Saintpaulia 'Red Sparkler'

Saintpaulia 'Snow Bunny'

Saintpaulia 'Tinted Clouds'

SANCHEZIA nobilis glaucophylla
Acanthaceae
Medium sunlight. Keep the soil moist. Medium humidity. Fertilize monthly and decrease to half doses during colder months. Propagate by seed or soft wood cuttings. Long, narrow leaves grow to 8 inches in length. Dark green coloring with contrasting primary veins and mid-rib of bright yellow. Center vein is reddish. The amount of sunlight provided will determine the strength of variegation. Attractive yellow flowers emerge from red bracts. Ecuador.

SANSEVIERIA trifasciata laurentii
"Variegated Snake Plant"
Liliaceae
Medium sunlight. Allow the soil to become slightly dry between waterings. Medium humidity. Fertilize with half doses and discontinue completely during colder months. Propagate by leaf cuttings or by division. Perhaps the most durable of all house plants. Very tolerant of all conditions. Most varieties have long, narrow succulent leaves that twist upward. Many are exotically banded and striped. A fast grower in sufficient sunlight. Two additional varieties are shown below.

Sansevieria trifasciata 'Hahnii'

Sansevieria trifasciata

132

SAXIFRAGA stolonifera
(S. sarmentosa)
"Strawberry Geranium"
Saxifragaceae
High sunlight. Allow the soil to become slightly dry between waterings. Medium humidity. Fertilize monthly. Propagate by runners. This is a lovely plant that when fully grown will measure no more than 6″ to 8″ across with 2″ leaves. It produces baby plants at the ends of delicate, long stems which may be used for propagation purposes or left on the plant to add to its charm. Native to Eastern Asia and Japan.

SAXIFRAGA stolonifera 'Tricolor'
(S. sarmentosa 'Tricolor')
"Magic Carpet"
Saxifragaceae
High sunlight. Allow the soil to become slightly dry between waterings. High humidity. Enjoys cooler locations down to 40 degrees. Fertilize monthly. Propagate by runners. Most commonly grown in hanging containers or in terrariums and dish gardens for added humidity. Beautiful foliage colors make this a popular yet somewhat more difficult to grow variety than the *"Strawberry Geranium"*.

SCHEFFLERA venulosa
Araliaceae
Medium sunlight. Keep the soil slightly moist and allow to become rather dry between waterings. Medium humidity. Fertilize monthly. Prefers warm temperatures to 80 degrees. Being a tree, this plant will not grow nearly as large in the home as it does in its natural habitat. Repot annually to encourage new growth. Use a fast draining soil mixture and do not overwater.

SCILLA violacea
"Silver Squill"
Liliaceae
Medium sunlight. Keep the soil moist. Medium humidity. Fertilize monthly. Propagate by seed or best by offsets. Thick leaved, bulbous based plant that is grown for both foliage and flowers. Silver mottling on moss colored leaves grows weak in insufficient sunlight. Tiny flowers grow on racemes high above foliage. Not commonly available in many nurseries. Native to Africa.

SCINDAPSUS aureus
(bot. RHAPHIDOPHORA aurea)
"Devils Ivy" or *"Golden Pothos"*
Araceae
Medium sunlight. Keep the soil slightly moist and allow to become rather dry between waterings. Medium humidity. Prefers warm areas. Propagate by soft wood cuttings. An attractive creeping or climbing vine. Good keeper, tolerating low sunlight conditions. If grown under ideal conditions, leaves can exceed well over a foot in length with stems of over 20 feet. Train on a moss stick or allow to trail.

SCINDAPSUS aureus 'Marble Queen'
(bot. RHAPIDOPHORA aurea)
"Marble Queen" or *"Taro Vine"*
Araceae
Medium sunlight. Keep the soil slightly moist and allow to become slightly dry between waterings. Medium humidity. Enjoys warm temperatures. Propagate by soft wood cuttings. Beautiful cream color splashed on a solid green background. Insufficient sunlight will cause less variegation in the foliage. Can be trained on a moss stick. A very tolerant mutation suitable for water culture.

SEDUM lineare 'Variegatum'
"Carpet Sedum"
Crassulaceae
Medium to high indirect sunlight. Allow the soil to become slightly dry between waterings. Low to medium humidity. Fertilize half doses monthly. Propagate by leaf cuttings, soft wood cuttings or by soil layering. Tiny, creeping stems are very densely clothed in small, to ⅞" long leaves. A fast growing ground cover that will mound over the sides of a container. Insufficient sunlight will cause slow, spindly growth. Yellow flowers.

SEDUM morganianum
"Donkey Tail" or *"Burro Tail"*
Crassulaceae
High sunlight. Keep the soil slightly moist. Use a fast draining soil mixture. Fertilize only every other month and discontinue in winter. Medium humidity. Propagate by leaf or soft wood cuttings. This curious plant requires abundant indirect sunlight to maintain healthy growth. It is a slow grower, but is capable of growing several feet long over a period of years. Use care when handling to avoid breaking off the fragile tassels. Native to Mexico.

SENECIO fulgens
"Scarlet kleinia"
Compositae
High sunlight. Allow the soil to become slightly moist between waterings. Medium humidity. Fertilize monthly. Propagate by soft wood cuttings or by dividing the tuberous root. Not an extremely common variety, yet available in some nurseries. Thick branching stems carry the fat, rubbery leaves. It eventually grows a gnarled, tuberous root stock. Red orange blooms grow high above the foliage. Native to Southern Africa.

SENECIO jacobsenii
"Weeping notonia" or "Weeping Jade"
Compositae
High sunlight. Keep the soil moist to slightly moist. Medium humidity. Fertilize half doses monthly. Propagate by soft wood cuttings or by soil layering. A very good variety with smooth, thick, rounded leaves and heavy flexible stems. Requires abundant sunlight to keep the foliage dense. Pinch back terminal growth for branching. Native to Eastern Africa.

SENECIO macroglossus
"Rubber Ivy"
Compositae
Medium sunlight. Keep the soil moist to slightly moist. Medium humidity. Fertilize monthly. Propagate easily by soft wood cuttings under a humid enclosure. Leaves and stems have a very rubbery, almost artificial consistency. The multi-pointed leaves are glossy and remain fresh in appearance. Pinch back terminal growth to keep full and branching. A hanging or pendant vine that will also twine on supports.

SENECIO macroglossus variegatus
"Variegated Rubber Ivy"
Compositae
Medium sunlight. Keep the soil moist to slightly moist. Medium humidity. Fertilize half doses monthly. Propagate by soft wood cuttings under a humid enclosure. A striking variety of *"Rubber Ivy"* requiring the same culture. Leaf margins are irregularly splashed with cream coloring. Becomes spindly if not occasionally pinched back or if grown in insufficient sunlight.

SENECIO mikanioides
"German Ivy"
Compositae
Medium sunlight. Keep the soil moist. Medium humidity. Fertilize monthly. Propagate by soft wood cuttings under a humid environment. Abundant, indirect sunlight will keep the foliage dense. Can be allowed to hang or trained on a trellis. Stems grow to 20 feet under ideal conditions. Good for water culture. Cut back if growth becomes spindly. Small yellow flowers in Winter. Native to South Africa.

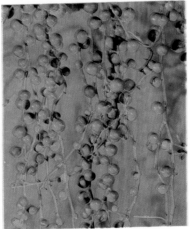

SENECIO rowleyanus
"String of Beads"
Compositae
High indirect sunlight. Allow the soil to become slightly dry between waterings. Medium humidity. Fertilize monthly. Propagate by soft wood cuttings or by soil layering. A small hanging succulent. Spherical leaves to ½ inch grow on stems to 8 feet long. White flowers. *S. herreianus* the *"Goose berry"* is slightly larger and leaves are more elongated. A very narrow lens, located on the side of each leaf, regulates amount of sunlight that enters the leaf.

SIDERASIS fuscata
"Brown Spiderwort"
Commelinaceae
Medium sunlight. Allow the soil to become slightly dry between waterings. Medium to high humidity. Fertilize monthly. Propagate by leaf and stem cuttings or by division with a mature specimen. Oval shaped leaves are covered with fuzzy, felt-like hairs. Silvery center stripe. Pretty, purple flowers peak out from inside foliage. Relative to the *"Wandering Jew."* Originally from Brazil.

SINNINGIA 'Doll Baby'
"Doll Baby"
Gesneriaceae
Medium sunlight. Keep the soil moist. Medium humidity. Fertilize half doses monthly. Propagate by seed, healthy stem and leaf cuttings or by dividing the tuber. Almost continuous light, purple slipper shaped flowers bloom on stems high above foliage. A small, to 3 inches across, miniature plant that can be successfully grown in the average home. Flowers keep for up to ten days.

SINNINGIA speciosa
"Gloxina"
Gesneriaceae
Medium sunlight. Keep the soil moist. Medium to high humidity. Fertilize half doses monthly. Propagate by seed, leaf and stem cuttings or by division of the tubers. Large velvety and usually bell shaped flowers are unmistakable. Large, wrinkled leaves have a fine, fuzzy covering. Usually grown from tubers, blooming 4 to 5 months after planting. When blooming ceases and growth stops, "wean" the pot dry. Let rest in a cool, dark location for 3 to 4 months.

SINNINGIA 'White Sprite'
"White Sprite"
Gesneriaceae
Medium sunlight. Keep the soil moist. High humidity. Fertilize monthly with very mild doses. Propagate by seed or by dividing the tubers. One of the most pleasing of all miniature plants. Perfectly shaped, white slipper flowers emerge almost continuously when grown in a humid environment. A one inch size pot is sufficient for a mature specimen. *S. pusilla* is the same with the exception of purple flowers. They may reseed themselves if undisturbed.

SPATHIPHYLLUM 'Clevelandii'
"White Flag"
Araceae
Medium sunlight. Keep the soil moist. Medium humidity. Fertilize monthly. Propagate by seed or by division. An evergreen plant that is grown for both foliage and flowers. Deep green, feather shaped leaves have indented veins and slightly rippled edges. Blooms on long, thin stems, consist of a spathe and spadix, similar to those of the *Philodendrons*. Foliage will tolerate low sunlight but blooming may be inhibited. Many other varieties from which to choose.

STREPTOCARPUS
"Cape Primroses"
Gesneriaceae
Medium sunlight. Keep the soil moist. Medium to high humidity. Fertilize half doses monthly. Propagate from seed, leaf cuttings or in some cases by division. A widely varied group of plants grown primarily for their long lasting trumpet shaped flowers. Leaves are slightly wrinkled and often finely haired. Indoors, under ideal conditions, blooming almost continuously. Some varieties only grow a single leaf. Hybrid seeds are readily available.

SYNGONIUM podophyllum
'Emerald Gem'

"Arrowhead Plant"
Araceae
Medium sunlight. Keep the soil moist. Medium humidity. Fertilize monthly. Propagate by rooting cuttings that include leaf nodes. A popular, all green variety with glossy, arrow head shaped leaves, to 6 inches long. Stems eventually become long and pendulous. As plant matures, the leaf joints or nodes will grow short, potential roots. These are easily visible and should be included in a cutting for successful propagation.

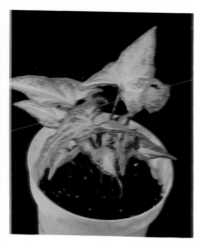

SYNGONIUM podophyllum
'Imperial White'
Araceae

Medium sunlight. Keep the soil moist. Medium humidity. Fertilize monthly. Propagate by rooting cuttings that include leaf nodes. A very pretty mutation that is almost completely white with an irregular, fresh green border. While growth is upright when very young, it will become pendulous or creeping when mature. Leaf lobes become rather divided as well, when older. *Syngoniums* will tolerate lower sunlight conditions, however, variegation may lessen.

SYNGONIUM podophyllum tricolor
"Tricolor Nephthytis"
Araceae

Medium sunlight. Keep the soil moist. Medium humidity. Fertilize monthly. Propagate by rooting cuttings that include leaf nodes. Unusual, very slender leaves are tri-lobed. Rarely exceeding 5 inches in length and having near white variegations in the veins that spread to the inner leaf. The margins are green. These plants may be allowed to hang or can be trained on moss sticks. Native to Costa Rica.

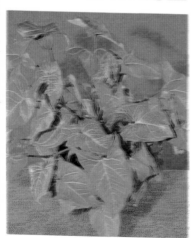

SYNGONIUM podophyllum
'Trileaf Wonder'
"Trileaf Wonder"
Araceae

Medium sunlight. Keep the soil moist. Medium humidity. Fertilize monthly. Propagate by rooting cuttings that include leaf nodes. Broad, arrow head shaped leaves are fresh green with very light green veins and midribs. Among the most popular of all varieties. Tolerant of lower sunlight and poor watering conditions. All varieties are excellent subjects for water culture.

TOLMIEA menziesii
"Piggyback Plant"
Saxifragaceae
Medium sunlight. Keep the soil moist. Medium humidity. Fertilize monthly. Propagate by leaf cuttings or leaf-stem cuttings. Prefers a light or "loose" soil mixture and also adapts well to water culture. This plant is unique in that it produces new leaves and stems right out of the bases of the older leaves. Dramatically wilts when soil is too dry but completely recovers if watered in time. Native to the United States, originating along the West Coast.

TRADESCANTIA fluminenis
'Variegata'
"Variegated Wandering Jew"
Commelinaceae
Medium sunlight. Allow the soil to become slightly dry between waterings. Medium humidity. Fertilize monthly. Propagate easily by soft wood cuttings. A striking hanging or trailing vine. The shiny leaves are beautifully striped with cream and green. A fast grower that tolerates most all adverse conditions. Pinch back occasionally, if desired, for fuller growth. Cuttings can be rooted and grown in water. South America.

TRADESCANTIA navicularis
"Chain Plant"
Commelinaceae
High sunlight. Allow the soil to become slightly dry between waterings. Medium humidity. Fertilize monthly. Propagate easily by soft wood cuttings. A small variety with green leaves to ¾ inch long. They are creased along the center and very glossy. The bases of the leaves almost completely surround the stem. Upright growth quickly becomes trailing or hanging with the weight of the foliage. Native to Peru.

TRADESCANTIA sillamontana
"White Velvet" or "White Gossamer"
Commelinaceae
High sunlight. Allow the soil to become slightly dry between waterings. Medium humidity. Fertilize monthly. Propagate easily by soft wood cuttings. A gorgeous trailer with dense foliage if grown in adequate sunlight. Alternating leaves, to 2 inches long, have a cotton like covering. Intense sunlight may cause the foliage to become reddish in color. Stems are pendulous. Pretty, light purple flowers. Native to Mexico.

ZEBRINA pendula 'Discolor'
"Tricolor Wandering Jew"
Commelinaceae
High sunlight. Allow the soil to become slightly dry between waterings. Medium humidity. Fertilize monthly. Propagate easily by soft wood cuttings. A lush and exotically colored hanging or trailing plant. The foam green leaves have a purple center stripe that is outlined with dark green. Purple edges and undersides. Leaves grow to 2½ inches long and are alternatingly set on thin, purple spotted stems. Variegation fades in insufficient sunlight.

ZEBRINA purpusii
"Bronze Wandering Jew"
Commelinaceae
High sunlight. Allow the soil to become slightly dry between waterings. Medium humidity. Fertilize monthly. Propagate easily by soft wood cuttings. A vigorous trailer that is most often grown in hanging containers. The lustrous, dark bronze leaves, to 2½ inches long, are lightly streaked with silvery green. Colors grow lighter in insufficient sunlight. Lavendar flowers in Autumn. A very durable and undemanding house plant. Native to Mexico.

PLANT ODDITIES

All cacti, and many succulents, have a special capacity to store water. Their ribbed or flattened body never turns a complete side to the sun. This is done so they can retain the precious water stored in their leaves. To keep from being eaten or trampled by animals they have adapted themselves with spines.

NEOREGELIA carolinae, *"Blushing Bromeliad"*—Classed as a succulent, a supply of water is stored not in its leaves but within a natural vase-like center formed by the foliage. In fact, as long as they can store water in this center funnel, they can survive long periods without roots. Its flower is hidden deep in the center surrounded by brilliant inner leaves.

SAXIFRAGA stolonifera, *"Strawberry Geranium"*—This lovely plant produces young plantlets at the end of long threadlike runners. The popular "Spider Plant" (CHLOROPHYTUM) produces runners in the same manner. These tiny plant babies can be removed and used for propagation or allowed to hang attractively below the "mother plant."

ORNITHOGALUM caudatum, *"Pregnant Onion"* or *"False Sea Onion"* — This unusual plant has a green bulb often over 5″ in diameter that sits above the soil. From this bulb grow long, drooping, strap-like leaves. Bulblets form along the side of the "mother bulb" and are used to propagate. The crushed leaves are used by the country people of Germany as a cauterizer for wounds.

MINOSA pudica, *"Sensitivity Plant"* —This is a most extraordinary plant in that at the slightest touch, its leaves will fold upward and the branches will collapse. This plant is actually a weed that grows throughout the tropics. It is easily grown on a window sill and will certainly fascinate children. It blooms with pretty pink pom-pom flowers.

TILLANDSIA, *(Bromeliad)* —These plants draw their required moisture from the air, their roots are used only to hold onto the host for support, not to obtain nourishment. They are often grown and displayed as a living mobile or mounted to a piece of wood. Their flowers are very showy and unique in appearance.

DARLINGTONIA californica, *"Cobra Plant,"* DIONAEA muscipula, *"Venus Fly Trap,"* SARRACENIA purpurea, *"Pitcher Plant"* —Carniverous plants are cultivated for their amazing capacity to catch and digest insects. They either close their traps, secrete deadly juices, reach out with sensitive sticky hairs or tentacles to attract and capture unwary insects.

IPOMOEA batatas, *"Sweet Potato"* —The common Sweet Potato, that is so widely eaten, can become an economical fast growing hanging plant. Use toothpicks to hold the Sweet Potato 2/3 out of a container of water. Roots form within a few days and foliage will soon follow. This can be a fun project for children.

MARANTA leuconeura kerchveana, *"Prayer Plant"* —In the evening this plant folds its oval leaves upward as if in prayer. Because of its beautiful foliage, the Prayer Plant has long been grown as a potted plant for the home. It also produces small white flowers, striped purple and is native to Brazil.

TOLMIEA menziesii, *"Piggyback Plant"* —This plant is unique because it produces new leaves and stems from the base of older leaves. The leaves themselves can be cut from the mother plant and rooted in soil or even a glass of water. The Piggyback is native to the Western United States.

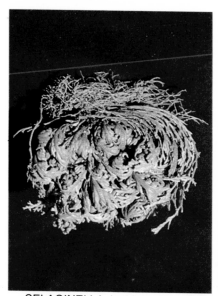

SELAGINELLA lepidophylla, *"Resurrection Plant"* —When this plant dries out, its branches curl into a tight ball and turn brown. When placed in water, the branches loosen and will unfold again, becoming a fresh emerald green. This characteristic remains even if the plant is dead.

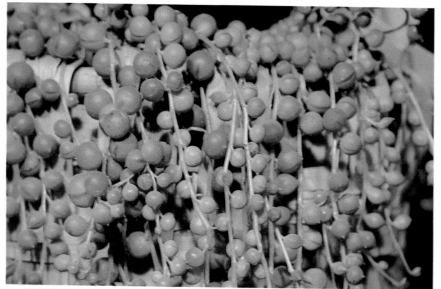

SENECIO rowleyanus, *"String of Beads"* —This small hanging succulent has spherical leaves with small slits on one side. The slits act as windows letting in the proper amount of sunlight. The stems can grow to 8′ in length and the leaves to ½″ in diameter. It also produces lovely white flowers.

INDEX BY COMMON NAME

INDEX BY COMMON NAME (cont.)

INDEX BY SCIENTIFIC NAME

INDEX BY SCIENTIFIC NAME (cont.)